ORIGINAL MOVIE
SCREENPLAY

Don Macpherson

TITAN BOOKS

THE AVENGERS
ORIGINAL MOVIE SCREENPLAY
ISBN 1 85286 932 1

Published by
Titan Books
42-44 Dolben Street
London SE1 0UP

First edition August 1998
10 9 8 7 6 5 4 3 2 1

The Avengers photographs by David Appleby and Matthew Rolston.

Titan would like to thank Susan Ekins, Aimee Chaille, Don Macpherson and Dave Rogers for all their help with this book.

British Library Cataloguing-in-Publication Data. A catalogue record for this book is available from the British Library.

Printed and bound in Great Britain by MPG, Victoria Square, Bodmin, Cornwall.

INTRODUCTION

An Interview
with Screenwriter
Don Macpherson

The blockbusting 1998 movie version of *The Avengers* has had a long journey to the big screen. Producer Jerry Weintraub originally bought the rights to the classic sixties television series back in 1987, and the project remained 'in development' until entering production a decade later. During that long period between 1987 and the cameras finally rolling at Pinewood Studios, many *Avengers* fans found themselves wondering how the eagerly awaited movie version would eventually turn out. But one fan knew already — because he'd written the script.

Screenwriter Don Macpherson has been an *Avengers* fan for years. Indeed, he was involved with the Wider TeleVision Access group, who during the seventies screened episodes from the original series at the Scala Cinema in London, the first time they had been shown on the big screen. His initial involvement with *The Avengers* movie began in the summer of 1993.

'I was in the archetypal position of being a screenwriter who hadn't had anything [original] made, but had a certain reputation and a certain prestige as being someone who could do something quite imaginative and quite bold that people could feel safe taking a risk with,' Macpherson explains, detailing his position in the movie industry at the time. 'I was working for a company at Warner Bros. and Jerry Weintraub, who had read my script for *Jonathan Wilde* [an adaptation of the Henry Fielding novel], which was very, very British, invited me to go in and see him. Quite naïve at the time, I had no idea really who Jerry was. I thought I was just going in because he liked the script and wanted to check me out. It wasn't long before we started talking about *The Avengers* — and I hadn't prepared anything. Fortunately, being a fan, I could speak with knowledge and enthusiasm about the show. Jerry wanted to know what the essentials of it were. I told him that over and above everything else, *The Avengers* was really a romance about an unconsummated love affair. That hit the spot. "And where do you think it takes place? Past, present or future?" I told him that it all took place in Avengersland. It's like the sixties, but as though the sixties had been going on for a very long time. It's the place where Steed and Emma live. It's a completely self-enclosed world. You could set it in the future, but it would still be the same: you just have to accept that the eighties never happened!

'Another thing I remember saying to him, because this was at a time when there were a lot of big, long movies happening, was that I didn't think that the film should be longer than 107 minutes. He really liked that, so we found a rapport. To my surprise, he then asked two Warner Bros. executives to join us, Billy Gerber and Lorenzo Di Bonaventura, and asked me to repeat what I'd told him. At the end of it, Jerry turned to them and said, "Are we doin' it or are we not?" They looked at one another, put their thumbs up and that was that. Jerry turned to me and said, "We're in!" That's Jerry Weintraub. He plays a hunch. If he's interested in something and he feels that you're not wasting his time — let's go! The interesting thing is, colleagues had been telling me for months that I'd be perfect for *The Avengers*, but I'd convinced myself that these things are actually sewn up and always go to the big boys.'

Macpherson had the job. Now all he needed was a story... 'There are two big dilemmas about working in Hollywood. One is *not* getting the job. The other one is *getting* the gig, because then you have to come up with the goods!' Five months after that initial meeting with Jerry Weintraub, the writer flew back to Hollywood, arriving with a rough storyline he'd put together while on the plane!

'When I say that I wrote it on the way to Los Angeles, I mean I scribbled down ideas and forced it into something that made sense, something that I thought was workable,' Macpherson recalls. 'I didn't actually have a story, just ideas for it. I remember writing it in reverse from the final scene, which at that time was set in the Siberian wastelands. I wrote everything back-wards in about eight hours. I landed at Los Angeles and the story editor, who knew I had something but was a little worried that I might not have any-thing good, was delighted when I was able to say, "I've got it." We spent a couple of weeks talking about it, adding a few things here, cutting a few things there. I think I delivered the first draft in May 1994, so essentially I was writing it between January and May. I didn't want to send it to Jerry unless people thought it was worth showing to him, of course, but Jerry got his hands on it the morning it arrived and read it before anyone else. I was told that he took it into his office and after a tense few moments they heard laughter coming from his room and he came out with a big smile.'

Macpherson's initial ideas took up twenty-four pages of hand-written notes. Taking the form of observations about the characters and world of *The Avengers* with some basic story ideas, it's fascinating to trace these early thoughts through to the finished screenplay. Here are a few excerpts:

Emma Peel:

> Widow — (heiress also). She is associated with: death, black leather, physically lethal, cerebral, witty, invulnerable, dutiful, questing —

EMMA IN LIFT
DESCENDS THROUGH
FRAME

Romantically alone, an English rose <u>without a man</u>.

John Steed:

    Devoted, remote, respectful, noble, loyal.

    Steed initially attracted to Emma: sees her as desirable, yet
sceptical of her: seeks to test her: to find out who she really is:
a little antagonism, witty wordplay and one-upmanship: takes
place in a series of <u>rescue bids</u>/<u>duels</u>.

Emma v. Steed:

    A battle of wits: <u>intrigue and attraction</u> why? what? how? Steed
respects her, but is hurt by her. A refusal of romance (At a cru-
cial point Steed has to realise that Emma will not be his) — —
This <u>sublimated</u> with adventure, thrills, risk, daring etc. gives
us the <u>sexiness</u>, the <u>kinkiness</u> and <u>perversity</u> of the movie —

V for Villain:

    <u>Threat</u> must not just be 'destroying the world' but <u>infernal, dia-
bolically clever, insinuating, terrifying</u> — villain should threat-
en <u>Mrs Peel</u>: he/she must have a secret 'in' to Emma's inner-
most fears and conflicts to place her in maximum jeopardy. NB
— in the <u>finale</u> — you only care about the <u>hero</u> getting to the
lever/dial/switch/failsafe device and the frustrations — crisis
— jeopardy there. — Nothing too technical or complicated — the
mechanics, by this stage, have to be irrelevant.

    In short — anything that detracts from the journey of the hero
to his/her goal is an irrelevance.

Countryside — stately homes, gardens, mazes & follies, hot air bal-
    loons + camera obscura.

City — capital, Victoria, alleys, river, imperial HQs & palace — run by
    custom and ritual, politeness and tea — preserving codes of
    behaviour: of the knight, of honour, of duty.

Avengersland is 60s — 90s — 21st century. Retro-modern, specific,
    fantastic — characters are English. (Steed's club: Emma would
    enter — the first woman to enter the steam room <u>ever</u> — i.e.
    into male preserve — up marble steps — then hall — down steps
    — through doors into T'Bath — — Steed naked.

A <u>romantic</u>, <u>erotic</u>, <u>dangerous</u>, landscape — things hidden, repressed by an apparent <u>order</u>... leading to subversion of that order — wild, surreal, playful, terror but also <u>simple</u>.

Movie clarity:

Story must unfold in easily understandable <u>visual</u> sequences — and <u>end</u> in a clear sequence of <u>inevitable</u> and <u>increasing physical momentum</u>. i.e. eliminate all extraneous plot and dialogue DM 1993.

'When you do a script like this, you have to be very certain when you start off that you want to carry it through,' notes Macpherson. 'In Hollywood, everyone has an opinion and people chip in with all sorts of ideas. The only thing you have as a writer, over and above your talent of putting words together, is concentration, focus and commitment. So unless you feel — have the arrogance to feel — that this is the one, this is the thing and it's yours, you won't really survive the course.'

After the first draft, only a few minor changes were made before the script was shown to the studio: 'The original script was so 'out there' and wild that there really wasn't much point in sitting around tinkering with it. The important thing was to have someone who wanted to commit to making it. I mean, when you have a script with Emma gatecrashing a Turkish bath, scientists dressed up as teddy bears and all these kind of outlandish things going on, you're fully committed to what it is; people aren't going to come in and say, "Mmm. I think we should change this..." Normally what happens is that these things go through a committee and get committeed to death.'

Happily, Macpherson's draft script was well received by the studio: 'They said that my script was the first one that had got 'it'... it was *The Avengers*, but it was modern, it was character driven and it had what was seen as the good things from the original [television series], but wasn't tied up with its own obsessions.'

One of the many 'good things' from the original series Macpherson adapted for his screenplay was, of course, the character of Emma Peel. In developing his take on Emma, Macpherson drew much from the television version (as portrayed by Diana Rigg), but also looked at the character that came before her — Steed's previous partner, Catherine Gale (played by Honor Blackman).

84

EMMA — LOOKING FOR THE BLACK TEDDYBEAR — TILT UP

BLACK TEDDY BEAR LEAPS ONTO EMMA.

'One of the strengths about the Emma Peel episodes was that they knew what to leave out, they didn't clutter it up too much with character,' comments Macpherson. 'In a movie you're looking for things which, even if you don't use them, you can use as a sort of backstory to the character. What I wanted to do was take the best of the myth of *The Avengers*, so certainly a lot of the Cathy Gale character was very important, up to a point. While her assertiveness, will and intellect were much to be admired, to me she seemed to be a little too independent, a little too in the driving seat and a little too invulnerable. At the same time there are two sides of Emma in a sense: she has this flirtatious, kittenish and playful element of verbal jousting, combined with total independence and lethal physicality. One of the things you're looking for when doing a movie is to try to find the right tone, the right balance between the characters, the male/female axis, because one of the witty elements of the whole *Avengers* thing is the way in which the male and female characters' attributes are shared out and reversed and played with. So I wanted a sort of mixture [of Catherine and Emma] essentially, but it's mainly Emma Peel who coloured my thinking.'

Having reached this stage, the project then sat in limbo until towards the end of 1995, when Jeremiah Chechik came on board as director. Even then, there was still a long way to go. 'We didn't actually know that the movie was going to be made until February 1996!' says Macpherson. 'The really good thing about Jerry Weintraub during that period was he never felt that he had to change the script in order to get people to commit. He was very relaxed about the whole thing and allowed me to get on with it. He said he wanted Steed and Emma, he wanted Mother and he wanted something *big* as the plot — something global, that was his brief. Obviously, he could intervene at any point. I talked to him at every single stage of the process, nothing happened without him knowing about it or being relayed to him, but he knows enough not to insist on something that is too detailed in the early stages, because you, the writer, have got to come up with it.'

The long period of development was put to good use, with Macpherson re-drafting the script several times. With Chechik as part of the team, the screenplay underwent some changes in approach. 'The earlier script we did was much darker in tone and much more intricately psychological,' Macpherson remembers. 'As a result, the villain was less clear, less single-minded, more maze-like. It was very much *The Avengers*, very interesting and absorbing, but for the scale of production we needed to do, someone had to give the call as to whether we could carry an audience through this particular maze. What Jeremiah brought to it was the sense that you had to simplify the villain, make him much clearer, in order to carry your audience. You could then make things more complicated, more *Avengers*-like. The idea was floated to change the original notion and I was very reluctant to let it go, until Jeremiah showed me that it was really quite simple to resolve. From that minute on it provided the intricacy required for *The Avengers*.'

Like most screenwriters, Macpherson had a 'dream cast' in mind for his lead characters when he was writing the script. Unlike most screenwriters, he was lucky enough to see the film made with that cast in place...

'When they started to look for Emma Peel, Uma was the first person Jerry went to, the one we really wanted was Uma Thurman — I say we in the knowledge that I had a certain conversational, thumbs up/thumbs down kind of input on these things, but I had no real say in the final casting, of course. The thing about my Emma Peel is that she has to be very intelligent, very brainy, very witty, very cool, very sensual, very sexual, but someone who is at ease with her sensuality, sexuality and intelligence — super intelligence. Sad but true, there are not many people who can do that on screen.

'This was back in '95 and obviously Uma wasn't as bankable then, nor was Ralph Fiennes, who was yet to make *The English Patient*. To me there were few British actors at a major league level who could play Steed, and I always thought that it had to be a serious actor, because the whole thing was so tongue in cheek anyway. What I liked in Ralph, apart from him being one of the best actors in the world, was that he has a certain steely quality and a certain wit. He's very masculine, but at the same time he isn't a kind of cliché-bound male. Patrick Macnee [the original Steed] came from a tradition that has almost gone. Ralph isn't from the same tradition but has more contemporary attributes which I think can be somewhat analogous to what Patrick brought to the role. To get one was wonderful. To get both was heaven sent. Uma certainly has qualities that are cinematically unique. She's very mysterious, very sensual, warm but unavailable, and it's very difficult to get people who register that on screen, as did Diana Rigg, who was incredibly vivacious, gorgeous, provocative and flirtatious, but essentially unavailable.

'In a screenwriting sense, all movies are love stories. They're either 'revenge' love stories or 'people-falling-in-love' love stories, so what you try to generate and create is what they formularise as U.S.T. — unresolved sexual tension, which I learned after I'd written this. In movie terms it means that you're really interested in people up to the point where they 'do it', and

...ROLLS OVER AND WE SEE ESKIMO EMMA'S
LEGS RUN INTO FIG.
    PAN UP TO HER FACE,

then you're not interested in them until they start falling out. If they are really in love and happily married, you have no interest in them dramatically, so a script tries to chart that. You want magnetic poles, but you want poles that are attracted to one another but dance around one another. That's the game I was trying to play, to try to get Uma and Ralph, both of whom are clever, sexy and funny, to dance around one another — then meet.'

And what of the villainous Sir August de Wynter? Macpherson was delighted with the actor — the icon — who was to bring him to life: 'The big thing with Sean Connery is, as soon as you lay eyes on him, you want to know what he's going to do next. You just put him on screen and you're moving — he is that threat! You don't need to explain it, you don't have to cut things out or add anything, you know that you're going to get what you need. Again, I never dreamed of having him in the movie and he was great for the part because he's never really done that kind of crazed, manic [character]. The other thing that was great from a creative side of things was that his particular brand of sexuality, authority and mischief works so well with Ralph and Uma. It was a great experience working with Sean and sculpting his part. He was so committed to it, he *was* Sir August de Wynter, two or three months before appearing on set.'

Writing a script for a 'stand alone' movie is a very different discipline from that of writing one episode of a long-running television series. There were several concerns that Macpherson needed to address in his screenplay: 'It's easy to get a story for *The Avengers*, but it's difficult I think to get a dramatic interest in the characters, because essentially Steed is Steed is Steed. Steed's whole appeal is that he is always like Steed. You don't really want to know that much more about him and he wants to preserve the mask. Emma Peel is complex, changeable, interesting, casting different sides to different people, so I always wanted her to be the dramatic focus for the [story], and Steed more the person trying to work out the enigma that is Emma Peel. So basically, Steed's mission, apart from saving the world, is to discover who *is* Emma Peel. From there my obsession was with the appeal of [the original *Avengers* television series episode] 'A Touch of Brimstone', which had a very wicked Emma. Now, whereas the nature of the piece means that you have to have Emma there solving the crime, I knew that we couldn't have her appearing on screen all the time. So the Bad Emma was literally coming up with someone who would be the bad side of Emma Peel and enable us to have more fun.'

Macpherson also had fun taking elements of the original series and including them in the script with a new twist. One moment of inspiration led to one of the film's highlights — the car chase.

'One of the nice, ordinary, staple sequences of *The Avengers* is the sequence where we see them driving in the car, so I wanted this in the movie, but something that had never been seen before, a car chase with a difference. Locked in my room one night, struggling for ideas, I was stumped. Then I heard 'The Flight of the Bumble Bee' on the radio. Bees, I thought, what about bees? The idea was stupid, and really kind of mad, of course, but bees, giant bees, chasing Emma and Steed and dive-bombing their car! Great idea, I thought, so in it went. You have no idea of how it's going to work, you don't even think about it, that's their problem. It wasn't fully worked through or anything, but as the people came in to do the storyboards, it became one of the things that was added to the plot. Jerry Weintraub liked the idea and insisted on keeping the bees in, to the point where it was going to take a lot of money, and the bees had to go. Then, halfway through, the bees were back! I'd written it so that it could be men in bee-like contraptions, or helicopters decked out in yellow and black stripes. When you write these things, of course, you don't care how they're going to do it, and have no interest in how much it is going to cost. The Invisible Jones thing, for instance. I thought that was going to be really cheap to do. But when you see how involved it becomes, it's frightening.'

The scene where Steed, looking for some answers, visits the office of the invisible Colonel Jones (voiced by Patrick Macnee) was written for a specific reason. 'Like a lot of the things you do, you do them intuitively and come up with the answers later, when you need them,' Macpherson elaborates. 'The way it happened was, I'd written this absolutely mad script. Now I'm going to deliver it to Jerry Weintraub, and the worst thing in a way is if he likes it then you're going to have to carry on with this crazy stuff, and you have no idea if anyone is going to understand what is going on.

'The most difficult part in the script is what you call the third quarter, the bit before the final act. It's the point where you've put these things all over the place and now you have to try to bring them all together. In ninety per cent of major movies, by the time this point happens, one has absolutely no idea at all as to what is happening! So, I created Invisible Jones, which seemed to me to be so simple, so funny and so very useful because I needed someone for Steed to go and see, *to tell him and the audience what was going on*! I wrote him as invisible, which was fitting and apt to *The Avengers* ethos — and who better to play him than Patrick Macnee, to have him be

EMMA TAKES EVASIVE
ACTION

BEES FIRE
CANONS

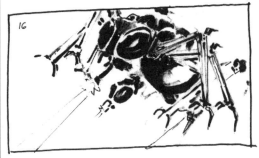

there but not there, as this sort of all-seeing, all-knowing guru. So it was written very much with him in mind.'

The refining of the screenplay was a constant process, ranging from minor dialogue rewrites (perhaps to better suit the style of the actor cast in a particular role) to more major changes, like the restructuring of an entire section of the story.

'The whole sequence of events from the scenes in Hallucinogen Hall to Steed and Emma arriving at the Serpentine was very difficult to land on in the right order,' Macpherson explains. 'We had sequences which people liked, but which were very busy and complicated. Originally, we had Steed and Emma escaping from Hallucinogen Hall in the balloon and they follow Bad Emma and Father in a helicopter. We changed the helicopter to the balloon, cut the balloon from one sequence and put it into another, which helped, but meant that we still had to figure out whether Steed and Emma go together or separately and whether Sir August captures Emma again in the finale. Jeremiah helped a great deal here by pointing out that the philosophical view is that you have to have everything resolved before they get back to their headquarters. The dilemma was mine. As a writer you always try to hedge your bets by throwing in as much as possible, so I originally had Sir August capturing Emma twice, but now he captures her once. What that does, of course, is throw every other scene slightly out of kilter, so we came up with a slightly more elaborate idea for the finale. Once you can feel that a certain sequence is working and is going to deliver what you need, you don't want to repeat it or have it refined or mirrored again towards the end. It's the same for Steed and Emma; you're in no doubt that she will find him attractive, he find her attractive and the mix will be intellectual and sexual enough. As soon as they set eyes on each other, you know that's going to work, so you can cut away to something else.'

Ultimately, Macpherson is happy to concede that he was just part of a team, the architect to builders Jerry Weintraub and Jeremiah Chechik. The collaboration was a happy one: 'Jeremiah has been totally committed to making the movie from day one. When he first came to the part where the scientists are dressed up as teddy bears, he said, "We're gonna have a lot of fun with this one." He would shoot it and we would see eye to eye — which is not always the case in this industry. We established this process where he'd come up with something, then I'd come up with something, and it was always the thing that he came up with which would be the *Avengers* notion. Once you have that, it goes through the whole [project]. He had several wonderful ideas. It's the same with the production designers. You see the stuff they've created and it's unbelievable. It's very, very British and at the same time very, very big.'

Very British, very big — over ten years in the making, it's a fitting description of *The Avengers* movie.

Don Macpherson was interviewed by Dave Rogers.

THE CAST

John Steed .... Ralph Fiennes

Emma Peel .... Uma Thurman

Sir August de Wynter .... Sean Connery

Mother .... Jim Broadbent

Father .... Fiona Shaw

Bailey .... Eddie Izzard

Brenda .... Carmen Ejogo

Dr Darling .... Nicholas Woodeson

Alice .... Eileen Atkins

Butler .... Michael Godley

Invisible Jones	Patrick Macnee
Trubshaw	John Wood
Boodle's Porter	Richard Lumsden
Messenger	Daniel Crowder
Tamara	Keeley Hawes
Tortured Scientist	Christopher Rozycki
World Council Ministers	Nadim Sawalha
	Christopher Godwin
	David Webbe
Donovan	Shaun Ryder

(The above credits are not all-inclusive and do not necessarily reflect final billing.)

THE SCREENPLAY

OPEN ON —

BLUE SKY WITH CLOUDS

PAN DOWN TO REVEAL:

EXT. DESERTED AIRSTRIP — DAY

A flat horizon, stretching to infinity.

A 180 degree pan reveals: nothing. Deserted, no hiding places. No animals, no humans, no objects. Except in mid distance —

RED PHONEBOX

brightly painted, traditional, comforting, belongs in a village green. Perfectly ordinary. Except for its location.

Silence. Only the wind over the plain. Except —

The PHONE RINGS.

RING-RING... *a mellow old fashioned tone. We wait for someone to answer it. But, of course, nothing and nobody for miles. Except —*

IN DISTANCE

a CAR ENGINE... *A puff of smoke on the horizon... Va-va-voom of high geared acceleration, as into view —*

ZOOM! ——————

CAR

speeding like a bullet. Driven at maximum, breakneck speed, 125 mph. A petite hard top E type Jaguar, all streamlined curves, full throttle, nears phonebox —

Screeches to a halt.

Dust clears, engine noise fades. From seat, hops —

EXT. DESERTED AIRSTRIP — PHONEBOX — DAY

A kinky boot in black leather.

Buckled. Strap at ankle. Crunching into the ground. PAN UP *to a beautiful woman, late 20s. In* CLOSE UPS *of —*

Tight black leather catsuit. A flash of auburn hair. Black leather like a second skin. Smoothed over legs, thighs. Buckled at wrists, straps at ankles, zips —

Pulled up over flesh. Sexual, invulnerable, cool. Very cool. She steps across to the phone. Picks up the receiver. Opens mouth. Doesn't even move her lips.

>   EMMA
> How now brown cow...?
>   *(Pause)*
> The quick brown fox jumped over
> the lazy dog —

SECURITY CAMERA

flicks on; swivelling head, she looks back into the lens. The distinctive leather, hair, eyes. Camera clicks, as —

>   VOICE (V/O)
>   *(From receiver; filtered)*
> Password affirmative. Press Button B.

She puts down receiver. Hangs a cardboard notice outside phonebox. Presses button B on the bakelite box. A coin from the slot. Then a HUM *as —*

INSIDE PHONEBOX —

floor lowers automatically. Her leather-clad figure disappears.

Hanging outside the box, a notice now reads 'Out Of Order'.

INT. PROSPERO PROGRAMME — LABORATORY

Underground. 'EMMA' descends on lift platform; steps into research lab in retro hi-tech. Walks past ASSISTANT, *down long steel corridors, Werner von Braun goes disco.*

About to pass thru door marked: 'Prospero Programme — Authorised Personnel Only'. Logo: lightning from cloud.

> INTERCOM
> *(Filtered voice)*
> Prospero Programme, phase five...
> weather conditions alpha-one...
> Wind speed zero-five... cloud
> patterns favorable...

AT DOOR —

A kindly, bespectacled PROFESSOR *recognizes her.*

> PROFESSOR
> Ah, Dr Peel.

She doesn't acknowledge. He runs to door.

> PROFESSOR
> I didn't expect you. I must have
> confused our schedule.

She moves down the corridor. He follows.

INT. PROSPERO PROGRAMME LABORATORY — CORRIDORS — DAY

Down corridors with air-lock doors: series of sealed chambers inside hi-tech labyrinth, 'Emma' walks, staring ahead, Professor beside. In b.g., countdown starts —

PROFESSOR
Are you alright...?
('Emma' ignores him)
I've just finished the analysis: one
microgram of anti-matter will
bring the cloud storms bang on
target —

At final airlock —

PROFESSOR
Only the control room down there —
('Emma' swivels round)
This way Dr Peel —
(Beat; something wrong)
... Dr Peel — ?

Suddenly INTO FOCUS, *without warning, leather-clad figure*

SLAMS

him against the wall. A karate blow to the neck kills the PROFESSOR
instantly. He slides down, as 'Emma' —

Steals his bunch of KEYS: *strange, cylindrical shapes.*

Walks away. Turns down the corridor marked 'NO ACCESS: TURN
BACK: RESTRICTED'. *She —*

PUNCHES

open doors. Heads down corridor.

INT. PROSPERO PROGRAMME — SECURITY HQ

ON MONITOR: *'Emma' down corridor. Security officer
responds —*

SECURITY OFFICER
Intruder in sector nine...

INT. PROSPERO PROGRAMME — GANTRY

'Emma' mounts gantry, two storys high, looking onto

HUGE GLASS BUBBLE

*Inside, weather storms fizz, crackle: black clouds spit rain —
lightning bolts flash — hurricane, winds blow — mushroom clouds
spout gases — snarling, raging* NOISE —

INTERCOM
(Filtered)
Radio transmitter on... Weather
antenna on... code systems, cloud
sensors on...

'Emma' reaches control area, where —

INT. PROSPERO PROGRAMME — CONTROL AREA

'Emma' unlocks KEYS: *pulls down: swooshing sound* HUMS —
HAND *on control lever — dials flicker — lights* FLASH *as she pushes
dials to max —*

Temperature gauge rises. CLOSE UP *— 'Emma' pushes dial past red
'danger' mark. Alarm sounds as —*

INTERCOM
(Filtered)
Intruder alert — Anti-matter levels
too high —

Numbers reconfigure — flashing message: 'CODE SYSTEM ALTERED'
Numbers whirl... ALARM. *Flashing sign* 'AUTO DESTRUCT' *Uh-oh...*

EXT. DESERTED AIRSTRIP — DAY

Up above ground, gantry raises up —

A radio TRANSMITTER *for weather antenna: silver blob, like a Koons sculpture. Sun glints off it.*

INSIDE GLASS BUBBLE —

weather patterns FIZZ *and* GROWL *like caged beasts —*

OVER *alarm rings as —*

IN CORRIDOR

GUARDS *race down to control room, and —*

ON GANTRY

'Emma' jumps down onto and through guards —

IN CORRIDOR

'Emma' rounds corner to see —

GUARDS *in attack formation, truncheons ready*

> GUARD
> Halt — !

'Emma' turns. GUARD *hesitates. 'Emma' suddenly swivels, somersaults —*

Wham — !! Killer double KICK *against two* GUARDS, *who go down, pivoting round as —*

Whhh — ! Whaaam !! Double scissor KICK *finish leaves two more* GUARDS *on floor. Without pausing, she* SPRINGS *back up, seemingly* FLOATING *against gravity, then —*

Lands like a cat, as OVER —

INTERCOM
(Filtered)
Auto-destruct countdown...
EVACUATE!!

Beep! Tell-tale whirr of CAMERA *snaps her — cool as ice.*

She walks out into AIRLOCK. CLOSE UP — EYES, *eerily gleaming, as —*

EXT./INT. DESERTED AIRSTRIP/LABORATORY — DAY

SWIRLING CLOUD *like a* TWISTER *full of crackling electronic energy floats menacingly towards antenna. From sky:*

LIGHTNING BOLT

hits antenna once, then... TWICE —

INSIDE LAB

Glass BUBBLE. *Inside, weather systems* FIZZ, CRACKLE *like ticking bombs. Glass splits, metals melt, about to —*

EXT. DESERTED AIRSTRIP — DAY

Boooooommmm!!!!

ON GROUND —

underground EXPLOSION *ripples skywards, tremors send waves of energy, mushroom cloud* BLAST *furls up to sky —*

Thundering organ music OVER, *as —*

INT. VILLAIN'S HEADQUARTERS — DAY

Passionate and powerful music plays INSIDE *magnificent vaulted cathedral-like space:*

A beautiful LIBRARY. TRACK DOWN *narrow aisle flanked by floor-to-ceiling books. Lead-stained windows, light streaming in, as —*

PAN OVER: *long tables laden with antique weather books, logs, a Magus's spells as —*

At end of library, TRACK THRU *ornate narrow archway, to* REVEAL:

A vast PIPE ORGAN. *As we* DOLLY CLOSER, PAN UP *to enormous 50ft pipes, music thundering, and* REVEAL *at base of organ, a solitary* MAN — PULL UP BEHIND — *our villain:* SIR AUGUST DE WYNTER

Rapt in concentration, he perches on seat, rocking and swaying.

As we approach, he turns, finally REVEAL:

SIR AUGUST

Mad, entranced by the music and his own passionate playing. As his fingers accelerate in virtuoso arpeggios, he finally SLAMS *the keyboard in a tingling vibrato, a final crashing note echoes —*

He stands up, and APPLAUDS *himself, gazing upwards. Breathless, a whispered howl:*

> SIR AUGUST
> Bravo. Let our revels begin...

ABOVE ORGAN — *is suspended a romantic, idealised portrait of the beautiful* EMMA PEEL. HOLD ON — SIR AUGUST's *demented, lovelorn stare, until —*

CRASH *of* MUSIC *begins cool 'Avengers' theme tune over —*

CREDITS SEQUENCE —

Bowler hat. Umbrella. Leather catsuit. Dandyish, erotic
SILHOUETTES *followed by* BLASTS *of violence, dreamy* OP-ART
puzzles, ticking clocks, psychedelic patterns over —

Sensuous BLACK *background — slowly revealed to be a woman's
leather-clad body: in silhouette — bowler hatted* STEED, *catsuited*
EMMA *in fetishistic detail...*

*Swish of legs, boots... hair tossed back — red nails over black...
creamy white skin... zips. Until, at the end: together in silhouette.
A jet black screen.*

PULL BACK *to* REVEAL...

DISSOLVE THRU TO:

EXT. VILLAGE — DAY

Brim of a BLACK BOWLER HAT.

*Outside cake shop, bell jangles. The hat's wearer exits, brisk, assured,
immaculate: Savile Row suit, stylish waistcoat, black —*

UMBRELLA *furled at side. Church* CLOCK *chimes* HOUR *— the
Beau Brummel dandy takes out fob watch, checks time.*

JOHN STEED

*our gentleman hero stands in narrow village street. All is well with
the world. A perfect day. Until from above:*

FLOWER VASE *drops. He sidesteps, vase smashes. Waving curtains at
upstairs window. Steed picks* CARNATION *for buttonhole, walks on.
A* VILLAGE POLICEMAN *emerges.*

STEED
Morning, constable.

He nods a polite greeting to Steed, then as he passes —

CHOP

deadly karate chop to Steed's back. Anticipating, Steed SWIRLS round, parries, thrusts to POLICEMAN, who FALLS to ground. Steed heads off, as if nothing had happened.

VILLAGERS pop up — MILKMAN breaks his bottles, threatening Steed with them, attack is quickly dispatched by Steed. Lady with pram (ALICE) emerges, throws knives, Steed ducks, which end up in a garage door — like a wave of commandos, suddenly from the garage doors come two chain welding auto mechanics who are quickly put down.

Up ahead, three NUNS walk across his path. As he passes a STREETSWEEPER —

> STEED
> Morning. Splendid day for a stroll...

He sees Nuns disappear into a pub. Decoys, leaving his back open to attack. Steed glimpses SHADOW, as —

CAR *skids round,* TOP SPEED, STRAIGHT FOR HIM — *nowhere to hide — no panic — pub sign overhead — Steed reaches UMBRELLA up — PULLS himself up — as car ZOOMS —*

SCREEECCHHH!! *Stops inches away.*

With STEED hanging by umbrella — MAN in white coat emerges from car, clicks stopwatch. Nods admiringly —

> DR DARLING
> Well done, Steed.

> STEED
> My pleasure.

Steed drops down, straightens lapel, picks up umbrella. With DR

DARLING, *turns final corner to* REVEAL —

INT. TEST AREA — OFFICE — DAY

Administration area with desks and phones. Bureaucrat with clip-board displays marks like skating judge. Steed checks 'village' is FAKE SET: *laboratory assault course.*

>   DR DARLING
>   You never can tell...

>   STEED
>   When the enemy will strike. If we
>   still have an enemy...

Dr Darling takes rubber stamp, stamps 'Top Secret' document bearing royal insignia and Ministry logo.

>   DR DARLING
>   Always an enemy, Steed. Just have
>   to know where to look...
>   *(Ominous)*
>   Something's up at The Ministry.
>   They want you to meet somebody.

>   STEED
>   They know where to find me.
>   *(Leaves ribboned box)*
>   Macaroons. For Mother...

Steed strides off, swinging furled brolly. Look up at clouds. Black bowler hat FILLS screen, on BLACK —

Plummy voice, on car RADIO:

>   ANNOUNCER (V/O)
>   ... An explosion devastated country-
>   side in Cambridgeshire, near a
>   science research establishment...

EXT. STREETS — LONDON — DAY

*Zoom! Steed's sleek green Bentley burns down deserted streets.
Backfiring like pistol shots. He drives thru —*

> ANNOUNCER (V/O)
> ... Meanwhile, the War Office
> confirmed the historic meeting of
> the World Council of Ministers will
> sign a new global defense treaty...

LONDON, 1999...

*This is 'Avengersland': parallel universe painted by Magritte, where
the sixties have never ended — they've just been going on for a very
long time. White stucco buildings. Regency style in candy colors.
Preserved in aspic, forever England —*

*No traffic. No extras. In this kinky pop world, nothing spoils the
view: sinister surreal De Chirico landscape of shadows. Car zooms
past, backfiring outside —*

EXT. EMMA PEEL'S FLAT — CHELSEA — DAY

OUTSIDE: *austere white stucco, identical Georgian houses.*

INT. EMMA PEEL'S FLAT — DAY

INSIDE: *a groovy, white space. Houses knocked into one ultra-
modern pad. Vast floor-to-ceiling heights decked with steel
walkways. Abstract, modern paintings. Glass tables, candy color
chairs.*

Buzzer rings. In BEDROOM *— The real* EMMA PEEL. *In bed.*

A cool, modern woman; expert, witty, vivacious. EMMA *throws off
sheets, gets up — stylish attire. She tick-tacks down metal walkways
to door.*

AT DOOR —

EMMA *flicks open automated eye, peers thru. Opens —*

IN CORRIDOR —

MESSENGER *hands over a package tied in a bow.*

> MESSENGER
>
> Dr Peel?

> EMMA
>
> Thank you.

EMMA *shuts door. Unties bow, opens — an embossed card:*

> EMMA
> *(Reading)*
> 'Please answer the telephone'.

EMMA *looks. Phone sits there. Just then...* RING-RING. EMMA *picks up. A recorded message, an upper-class woman's voice like the old 'speaking clock':*

> WOMAN (O.S.)
> *(Filtered)*
> Boodle's 2.30pm. Mr John Steed...
> Boodle's 2.30pm. Mr John Steed...

BEEP. *Phone goes dead.* EMMA *looks at the case: a box of chocs. Puzzled, she pops one in mouth —*

EXT. BOODLE'S — PALL MALL — DAY

Outside white stucco buildings, distinctive powder blue Jaguar pulls up, parks. News vendor's ad reads:

'MYSTERIOUS EXPLOSION: DEFENCE ALERT'.

Out gets EMMA PEEL. *Different attire. She climbs steps. She goes in, past an astonished uniformed* COMMISSIONAIRE.

INT. BOODLE'S LOBBY — CONTINUOUS ACTION

A young PORTER *approaches her, equally surprised.*

> PORTER
> May I help you, madam...?

> EMMA
> For Mr John Steed. I'm Dr Peel.

> PORTER
> I'm afraid that's impossible.

He points to notice: 'No non-members. No animals. No women.'

> PORTER
> You are female?

> EMMA
> As you see.

> PORTER
> Then you can't come in.

> EMMA
> I have an appointment.

> PORTER
> No women. Not in Boodles. Not
> since 1762.

> EMMA
> Really — what happened in 1762?

Emma breezes past, already inside hall. Old mahogany, leather chairs. A male enclave.

The PORTER *lunges at her. She side steps with a delicate ju-jitsu move, sending him tumbling down the stairs.*

> EMMA
> Thank you so much. I can find Mr
> Steed myself.

— collapses on the ground in agony. EMMA *ignores him. Pushes thru double doors, upstairs, statues of naked bronze warriors frown down on her, into —*

INT. BOODLE'S — LIBRARY — DAY

A silent hall of learning, elegant bookcases wall to ceiling. EMMA *walks calmly thru chairs and tables, past fusty relics of* MEMBERS, *one of whom audibly —*

Gasps... as EMMA *tick-tacks past, into —*

INT. BOODLE'S — TURKISH BATHS — DAY

Thru a cloud of steam in an oriental room —

STEED *sits naked, save for towel — bowler at side. Reads weather forecast below story about a 'mysterious explosion'. He hears a disturbance, thru mist, sees —*

EMMA *before him.*

> STEED
> ... Doctor Peel, I presume?

> EMMA
> And you must be Steed. Please
> don't get up.

He doesn't. HISSING STEAM *between them as they study.*

STEED
I was about to throw in the towel.

EMMA
Sorry. A spot of bother at the door.

STEED
I shouldn't wonder. Not a woman
inside Boodles since —

EMMA
1762. Until you invited me here.
(Looks around)
So what was all this — some sort of
test?

STEED
Congratulations. You've entered a
bastion of male privilege. You aren't
someone who plays by the rules,
Doctor.

EMMA
Rules are made to be broken.

STEED
Not by me. Play by the rules,
Doctor. Or the game is nothing.

EMMA
And just what is the game?

STEED
I say, this is all terribly formal.
Must I go on calling you Dr Peel?

EMMA
Under the circumstances, you may
call me Mrs Peel.

STEED
        Much better.

                    EMMA
        Now that we've settled the matter
        of titles, will you kindly explain
        why you wished to meet me?

                    STEED
        I didn't. Mother did.

                    EMMA
        Mother?

                    STEED
        Mother.

The chimes of Big Ben ring out, as —

EXT. TRAFALGAR SQUARE — DAY

Bong... PULL BACK *to —* BIG BEN's *gothic clocktower, staring down
at empty streets below.* CAR ROAR OVER —

Down Embankment, sleek Bentley zooms. STEED *drives,* EMMA *cool
as a cucumber.*

                    STEED
        Four o'clock. Mustn't be late.

                    EMMA
        Time for tea?

                    STEED
        A word of warning. Don't take the
        macaroon. Mother's favourite.

EXT. MINISTRY UNDERGROUND ENTRANCE — DAY

STEED *swerves into secret car park entrance by riverbank. He pulls up before sign —*

THAMES RIVER AUTHORITY
No Admittance

AT CONTROL BARRIER — STEED *inserts card. Light flashes: 'Security — Top Priority Clearance Only'. Barrier lifts.* EMMA *looks at* STEED, *reappraising him as Big Ben chimes. Car disappears in darkness...*

INT. 'MINISTRY' SECRET SERVICE HQ — UNDERWATER — DAY

Darkness. A flash of light as 8mm projector flickers —

Scratchy b/w Ministry film of scientific evidence: cows on parched scrub, lawn bowlers in snowdrift. Spooky, deadpan, surreal. OVER: *a man's voice.*

> MOTHER (O.S.)
> *(In silhouette)*
> At first it was the Chew Lakes
> evaporating, then Kent pastureland
> turning overnight into African
> scrub. A whole series of bizarre
> weather reports...

In shadow, Steed and Emma watch wall screen:

IN SILHOUETTE: MOTHER — *a man in wheelchair, continues:*

> MOTHER
> One Surrey village recorded victims
> of sunburn and frostbite on the
> same day. Freak temperatures of
> 150 degrees.

> EMMA
> *(Unimpressed)*
> Well?

> MOTHER
> On the hottest day of the year, half
> its football team froze to death.

> EMMA
> Time to get your woolens.

> MOTHER
> The weather's turning nasty —

> EMMA
> *(Unimpressed)*
> No discernible pattern. We were
> tracking all these reports at the
> lab —

> MOTHER
> We went further. Sent our best
> scientists into the field. Most are
> missing... or dead.

ON SCREEN: *macabre death tableaux — man trapped in ice; body spontaneously combusted; agent in dry riverbed of dead fish.*

BEHIND WALL

secret video screens monitor EMMA's *reactions* —

> MOTHER
> Frankly, we're baffled. The
> weather's changing. Fast. We
> want to know why...

> STEED
> Natural phenomenon — ... Or man
> made?

EMMA
That about covers it.

MOTHER *wheels himself in front of screen: beam illuminates his features — slicked hair, bluffly sinister, as —*

MOTHER
Exactly. The Prospero Programme.

ON SCREEN: *flash of Prospero devastation — lights up.*

LARGE SCREEN ROLLS UP...

revealing water. We are beneath the Thames — WIDEN to reveal... BRENDA, *pulling curtain cord. Wheels himself round.*

MOTHER, STEED, *and* EMMA *sitting together —*

MOTHER
I always prefer a room with a view,
don't you?
                    (Picks up teapot)
Tea? I'll be Mother...

MOTHER *pours. REVEAL HQ of The Ministry, elite intelligence force in subterranean bureaucracy, wooden walkways over leaking puddles.*

EMMA
I know about the Prospero
Programme explosion... Sugar. One
lump... Is that why I'm here...?

MOTHER
You're here for tea, Mrs Peel...

BRENDA (O.S.)
Welcome to The Ministry.
Macaroon?

BRENDA, *Mother's bodyguard — glam leather-clad Moneypenny —*
wheels cake trolley over. Emma takes macaroon.

> STEED
> Prospero... Shakespearean
> Magician. Do explain.

> EMMA
> Top secret research. A government
> project I was working on to create a
> weather shield.
> > *(For Steed)*
> A defensive umbrella.

> STEED
> Ah... I get it. Someone attacks... we
> put up this umbrella... everyone
> goes home for tea. Marvellous.

> MOTHER
> Until someone blows up the
> research lab —

> STEED
> Did they just walk in? How did they
> get past security?

> MOTHER
> That's what's interesting. Security
> cameras at the Prospero lab picked
> up a picture during the attack...
> There's something I'd like you to
> see — if you have a moment...

ON HIDDEN SCREENS: *video* CLOSE UPS — EMMA's *reactions*
dissected.

CUT TO:

At desk, using keyboard MOTHER *summons up surveillance images on screen,* STEED *and* EMMA *look on. Shock-on-screen face of* EMMA PEEL.

>STEED
>She looks terribly familiar.

EMMA *stares at* PHOTO *on screen. Incredible, like a twin sister.*

>MOTHER
>This is a special assignment. With a twist. You're our chief suspect.

>EMMA
>I'm innocent... of course.

>STEED
>Or guilty until proven innocent.

>EMMA
>Why would I sabotage my own project?

>MOTHER
>You tell us.

>EMMA
>That looks like me. But it can't be.

Steed looks back to Mother. Who presses button, tape switches on:

>MOTHER
>*(Lets tape play)*
>We received a communiqué...
>Anonymous, of course...

>VOICE
>*(Recorded filtered voice)*
>"... Act One begins with a tempest, one of Prospero's powers. A fine performance by Mrs Peel. One the

Council of Ministers will soon
admire..." — (CLICK)

Steed watches Emma listen. Mother switches off.

> MOTHER
> You'll be allowed a privilege: to
> prove your innocence.

> EMMA
> To be precise, you're saying I have
> no choice.

> MOTHER
> The World Council of Ministers is
> meeting next week to sign a treaty.
> We don't have much time. Find out
> what's going on. And quickly...

Steed turns to Emma, they rise to go. On way to door —

> STEED
> Mother wants me to show you the
> ropes. He'd like us to work as a
> team.

> EMMA
> You mean, I have to trust you.

> STEED
> Absolutely, Mrs Peel. At your beck
> and call. Shall we...?

Emma looks at him... deadly. BRENDA *escorts them out, exiting as* MOTHER *takes a cigarette out of pocket and lights it —*

FROM SECRET DOOR

with DR DARLING, FATHER *(a woman) emerges. Elegant, dark glasses, wired with earpiece, Mother's second-in-command is also... blind.*

MOTHER
Think she killed those scientists,
Father?

FATHER
All in my report, Mother.

MOTHER
Why haven't I read it?

FATHER
Because I haven't given it to you.
My theory goes Mrs Peel may be
ill...

Mother looks up from walls of files.

MOTHER
... Amnesia? Hypnosis?

FATHER
Possibly. Split personality, maybe
trauma. There was a husband...
            (Mother takes note)
Test pilot, missing over the
Amazon. Presumed dead. He was
one of ours —

MOTHER
Revenge is a possible motive —

FATHER
She certainly fits our profile —

MOTHER
Mrs Peel's our only lead. Either
she'll lead us to the real enemy. Or
they'll find her.

FATHER

She knows too much. May be a
risk. Admit it, Mother. If she is,
there's only one solution...
(At Mother)
... Termination.

CLASHING BLADES OVER...

EMMA (O.S.)

... The Prospero Programme was
very simple...

INT. TRUBSHAW'S OUTFITTERS — DAY

In upper balcony of Trubshaw's, where —

*Steed and Emma (new outfit), cross swords, testing new blades. Like
everything she does, Emma is a champion. Tic-tac...*

EMMA

... We were bombarding protons
and ions to make anti-matter...

STEED

I better start calling you 'doctor'
again... Weight on the back foot...

Tic-tac-tic...

EMMA

... Artificially creating new weather
systems...

STEED

You're a lady of hidden talents, Mrs
Peel... a little more flexibility in the
wrist...

Tic-tac-tic-tac...

> STEED
> Scientist...
> > *(Tic-tac)*
> ... swordsman...
> > *(Tic-tac)*
> ... To what do you attribute your
> overachievements?

Fast swordplay. Tic-tac-tic-tac-tic. Steed's good too.

> EMMA
> My father always wanted a boy.

> STEED
> Really? I fail to see the connection.

> EMMA
> I had a feeling you would. So did
> he.

She lunges; foil tips right into heart on Steed's chest.

> TRUBSHAW (O.S.)
> Touché.

*REVEAL: Trubshaw, a gentleman's gentleman. Swissh! Steed weighs
weapon like knight. Emma hands over blade. Reveal samurai-like
display of umbrellas and swordsticks:*

> STEED
> The ebony handles are a touch
> heavy. I'll stick to the rosewood.

> TRUBSHAW
> The solid crook? Excellent, sir. If
> you'll walk this way...

DOWNSTAIRS

old-fashioned outfitters: hunting trophies, attendants in tails, wing-collars. Emma breezes thru, flirtatiously —

> EMMA
> Now my knight has chosen his
> armor, shouldn't we be on our way?

> STEED
> Trubshaw's a man worth meeting.
> No point in setting out half-shod.
> That's why I ordered you a pair of
> boots, Mrs Peel...

> EMMA
> Thank you.

> TRUBSHAW
> Madam will appreciate our expertise
> in leather...

Trubshaw fits Steed's waistcoat; Emma fiddles with ties.

> EMMA
> Old school ties. How quaint. One of
> yours?

> STEED
> Tradition is all we have, Mrs Peel.

> TRUBSHAW
> I hope your shoes and waistcoat
> please, sir.

> STEED
> Impeccable.

TRUBSHAW
Quite. Your items will be delivered
to the usual address...
(Beat)
Mrs Peel's boots?

STEED
Send them on.

TRUBSHAW *exits.* STEED *adjusts in new waistcoat.*

STEED
Perfect fit. You'll appreciate
Trubshaw's boots.

EMMA
I hope so. I'm very particular.

STEED
So I'd gathered.

EXT. TRUBSHAW'S OUTFITTERS — JERMYN STREET — DAY

Outside in street, eyes watching Emma and Steed exit...

STEED
Mother suggested we go for a spin.

EMMA
Do you always listen to Mother?

STEED
That depends. Marvellous weather.
Not the sort of day to be stuck in
town. We ought to get away.

EMMA
'We'?

> STEED
> Yes. Just the two of us. A weekend
> in the country. Long walks, wind in
> your hair. How about it, Mrs Peel?

> EMMA
> Depends what you have in mind.

> STEED
> I'm a nature lover. So whatever
> comes naturally. Shall we take my
> car?

They hop into Bentley. Steed turns ignition, car won't start.

> STEED
> ... Most odd.

> EMMA
> Rusty, perhaps.

> STEED
> Hope I haven't lost the knack.

Steed coaxes throttle, motor revs... Rrrmmm! Ignition! Steed's Bentley zooms off, mach speed —

REVEAL — youngish man in black polo neck, Beatle mop, pouting lips. BAILEY, a cool psychopath. With his BULLY BOYS. He watches Steed and Emma zoom off, as —

INT. VILLAIN'S HQ — DAY

A musical BATON

Twirls, conducting massed choirs of recorded angelic voices in exquisite harmony...

IN SHADOW: *an enigmatic* FURRY *silhouette wields baton, swaying rhythmically, as...*

INSIDE *spooky mirrored chamber, the eerie music plays. Mirrors reflect to infinity, as above special couch —*

SPIRAL HYPNODISC

whirrs trippy psychedelic patterns to a throbbing pulse. On couch with straps and head clamp, infinite patterns confuse and coerce —

> SCIENTIST (O.S.)
> *(Groaning in pain)*
> Nnnnn... Urrr... Nnnn-ooo...

Circle round, creep up on couch. On which lies... a pebble-glassed, egghead SCIENTIST, *moaning a little too loudly, for...*

FROM SHADOWS, REVEAL *furry silhouette turns of...*

A giant TEDDY BEAR.

Man-sized. Music loving. Baton twirling. In stylish tartan teddy bear suit. Waving ruby-handled BATON *with razor-sharp point —*

The TEDDY *conducts vigorously to music blasting out from floor to ceiling speakers, as if his life depended upon it. His victim's moans grow louder. Until, irritated by moans —*

> TARTAN TEDDY
> So bloody tiresome —

The TARTAN TEDDY *loses patience. Pointing his* BATON *at the* SCIENTIST, *he stretches out paw — and in tune with music —*

Whoosh! Rhythmically cuts and slashes victim's cheeks with jewelled BATON, *drawing beads of blood, until —*

Ping! Whacks SCIENTIST *on nose!*

TARTAN TEDDY
You know what I want to know...

Ouch! The TARTAN TEDDY *kicks machine. Which whirrs faster. On couch,* SCIENTIST *finally gives in. Shaking helplessly, he starts to mumble his secrets...*

SCIENTIST
(In b.g.)
... In the production of anti-matter,
the ratio of protons to ions...

SIR AUGUST
(Singing)
Protons to ions...

SCIENTIST
... is equal to the mass of cloud
pressure calculated by the Fermetti
principle, using 'e' as the base...

SIR AUGUST
'E' as the base...

Meanwhile, our TARTAN TEDDY *villain listens contentedly. Relishing the intense choral music which soars majestically, until —
With bullfighter's flourish, he stands over his* SCIENTIST, RAISES *the* BATON, *razor-point flashing in light —*

And on an elegiac climax, soaring violins —

PLUNGES *it down.*

STEED (O.S.)
Press that button, would you? Tea?

DISSOLVE THRU TO:

EXT. COUNTRYSIDE — ROADS — DAY

Steed and Emma zoom past in his Bentley...

CLOSE UP — SPECIAL DASHBOARD COMPARTMENT

Opens, revealing tea service: samovar of tea, feeding into pot, pouring into china cups... WIDEN to reveal:

INT. BENTLEY — DAY

> EMMA
> Is the pot warm?

> STEED
> Always.

> EMMA
> Milk?

> STEED
> Lemon. Just a twist.

Corrected, Emma pours from the samovar...

> STEED
> No cakes. You don't mind roughing
> it, do you?

> EMMA
> On the contrary. But shouldn't we
> be making plans for tonight?

> STEED
> We are. Thought we'd have time to
> pay a social visit. Since we
> happened to be passing.

> EMMA
> I thought as much. Anyone in
> particular?

> STEED
> Sir August De Wynter. Former
> Ministry man. Head of Special
> Projects, ran our Strategic
> Deception Initiative. He's retired
> now. Very rich, very odd...

> EMMA
> Hmmmm... Intriguing. A wealthy
> recluse...?

STEED *looks in mirror. Behind them, a car. Trailing?*

He puts his foot down. Zoom...

EXT. COUNTRYSIDE/ INT. BENTLEY — DAY

The BENTLEY ROARS *by — then other car — Bailey trailing. Inside Bentley, Steed with Emma.*

> STEED
> ... More interesting than that. Sir
> August's a fanatical meteorologist.
> Runs in the family. Mother called
> April. Sisters — May, June...

> EMMA
> July... August? The family does
> seem to have weather on the
> brain... Any other vices?

> STEED
> All of a piece, really. Sir August's
> chairman of BROLLY...
> > *(Off her look)*

British Royal Organization for
Lasting Liquid Years. A private
group recruiting top scientists.
Thinks British weather has been
tampered with by... aliens. All very
hush-hush. Not too keen on him at
The Ministry. Mother tells me he
left under —

                    EMMA
A cloud...?

                    STEED
Naturally. If it wouldn't be too
much bother, could you charm him
a little?

                    EMMA
I'll see what I can do.

                    STEED
... More tea?

                    EMMA
No thanks.

                    STEED
I meant me.

EXT. 'HALLUCINOGEN HALL' — DAY

Ahead, open main gates. A vast, strange house with towers and turrets. They stop at gate.

                    STEED
I'll snoop around. You distract him.

                    EMMA
How?

STEED

Try small talk...

EMMA

... The weather?

STEED

Maybe something more feminine.
A woman's touch...
                 (Off Emma's look)
That should do the trick.

EMMA

Think so? Your confidence is
overwhelming.

STEED

Such modesty.

EMMA

A minor talent. Or hadn't you
noticed?

*Steed drops Emma off. She walks into courtyard. He sets off to
explore. Emma walks past a mechanical peacock, fans tail, CLICKS
with WHIRR of CAMERA...*

EXT. 'HALLUCINOGEN HALL' — ENTRANCE — DAY

As Emma climbs steps, reveals BAILEY watching —

EXT. 'HALLUCINOGEN HALL' — DOORWAY — DAY

Emma is greeted by a BUTLER, she enters.

INT. 'HALLUCINOGEN HALL' — CORRIDORS — DAY

They head down a hallway, he hands her an umbrella. No explanation. She acknowledges politely —

> EMMA
>
> Thank you.

Emma follows BUTLER *down corridor, garlanded with strange plants and flowers. She notices a pair of sensuous, oversized orchids:*

> EMMA
> *(Re: plants)*
>
> Curious...

> BUTLER
>
> Yes, miss.

> EMMA
>
> Missus.

At end of corridor, EMMA *sees double doors: from which sound of* OPERA *echoes loudly. Curious,* EMMA *heads closer.* TRACK DOWN *— towards, until —*

BUTLER *opens doors, letting* EMMA *into —*

INT. 'HALLUCINOGEN HALL' — CONSERVATORY — DAY

The sound of Pavarotti swells to ear-splitting pitch inside a vast conservatory, that resembles...

An indoor RAIN FOREST.

Plants. Trees. Creepers. Misting RAIN *like a tropical monsoon.* THUNDER *rolls, as —*

> EMMA
>
> Hello...?

No reply. Only singing as EMMA stalks her prey, a big game hunter armed only with umbrella, sees:

IN 'JUNGLE', *ahead* — SHADOWY FIGURE *cast large on a wall, spinning wildly like a dervish — singing along — slightly off — to a seductive Puccini aria —*

> SIR AUGUST (O.S.)
> *(Singing to Puccini)*
> "...Talor dal mio forziere
> Ruban tutti I gioielli
> Due ladri: gli occhi belli..."

INSIDE RAINFOREST*: EMMA pops umbrella up, pushes past branches, fearlessly into heart of darkness —*

From behind, a rustle of bushes — Emma pushes back, knocking into something — A hand reaches up like a serpent round her neck —

Startled, she swivels round to see — Handsome, charismatic man —

REVEAL*: SIR AUGUST in rain and mist —*

> SIR AUGUST
> Peel... Emma Peel.

Thunder ROLLS, *lightning* FLASHES, *illuminating* — His glinting EYES. *Wicked smile.*

> EMMA
> You're all wet.
> *(Beat)*
> Have we met? Or is it just the rain
> that's familiar?

He moves under her umbrella. Their EYES LOCKED *together —*

Lightning strikes. A moment for Emma to recover —

SIR AUGUST
We share a passion, I believe.
(Kisses her hand)
I always admire a woman who's
meteorologically inclined —

EMMA
Mutual, I'm sure. The thrill of the
monsoon —

SIR AUGUST
Oh yes... Monsoons... Even as a boy,
when Nanna taught me the naming
of clouds...

EMMA
Cumulus...
(Sir A: Yes...)
Strato-cumulus...
(Sir A: Oh, yes...)
Nimbus...

SIR AUGUST *throws* EMMA's *umbrella away.*

SIR AUGUST
I discovered then, nothing beats a
good lashing. Take India — you can
have a good ten inches overnight.

SIR AUGUST *leads* EMMA *out of rain. Watched from rainforest by*
POV: *silhouetted onlooker.*

SIR AUGUST
Come this way...
(Beat)
One should never fear being wet.

EXT. HALLUCINOGEN HALL — COUNTRYSIDE — DAY

Out in countryside, something fishy.

STEED *heads off for distant red phonebox, as —*

INT. HALLUCINOGEN HALL — CONSERVATORY — DAY

Out of the rain, in a different part of rainforest, SIR AUGUST *and* EMMA *towel off. He moves closer —*

>   SIR AUGUST
>   Let me give you a hand...

Behind her, Sir August eagerly rubs Emma's hair dry. In a seductive dance, his strong arms embrace her, delicately patting —

>   EMMA
>   These rapid climate changes. The
>   Ministry needs some answers.

>   SIR AUGUST
>   *(In disgust)*
>   The Ministry...

>   EMMA
>   Do you mind...?

>   SIR AUGUST
>   *(To himself)*
>   I wouldn't mind anything with you.
>   *(To Emma)*
>   Very well.

As Emma talks, Sir August moves from drying her hair, to wistful inspection: smelling, caressing, slowly intoxicated by her —

>   EMMA
>   I need a specialist opinion.

Theoretically speaking, if I wanted
to alter cloud patterns, how would
I power it?
*(Emma tries to concentrate, as Sir A moves
down to her knees)*
By micro-transmission...?

SIR AUGUST
Oh, yes... micro-transmission...

EMMA
... I've been thinking. The military
applications were never looked
into. After the cold war —

SIR AUGUST
The hot and cold war...

EMMA
An outdated theory. Intriguing but
impossible.

SIR AUGUST
Nothing's impossible. Only
mathematically improbable, my
dear Dr Peel —

EMMA
(Breaking off curtly)
Dry enough, don't you think?

*Emma unravels herself, as Sir August leads her to his prize orchids,
under huge magnifiers.*

SIR AUGUST
(Pointing)
Look here. The twisted labellum.
Note the upturned apiculus on the
dorsal sepal. A genetic impossibility.
This flower should not exist. Yet

here it is. I did it. Beautiful, no...?
(He strokes it)
Touch it, Dr Peel.

SIR AUGUST

EMMA

I feel I'm wasting my time.

SIR AUGUST

Please. Touch it...

EMMA

Sorry to trouble you. It's obvious
you know nothing —

*Emma's remark stings him. Old resentments and scorn flood back,
rage boils over —*

SIR AUGUST
(Venting)
I know nothing — ? I have forgotten
more than those fools at The
Ministry ever knew. The ratio of
protons to ions? Me... The entire
micro-transmission theory? Me... I
did it all. My way. They said I was
mad...

Bam! Thru doors, BUTLER pushes tea trolley.

SIR AUGUST

Tea?

*Butler whispers to Sir August, as Emma walks over to him by
window. He pours, staring out at rain —*

SIR AUGUST
Perhaps your friend would like to
join us?

He turns. A feral look, catching her off guard.

> EMMA
> My friend — ?

> SIR AUGUST
> Hmm. Some very nasty weather
> about.

> EMMA
> Ah... Perhaps he's lost.

> SIR AUGUST
> I don't think so. We don't get many
> trespassers up here.

> EMMA
> Why?

> SIR AUGUST
> We shoot them.
> *(Beat)*
> Sugar?

SIR AUGUST *gazes out of window.* EMMA *looks out —*

EXT. COUNTRYSIDE — DAY

Beneath sign: 'NO TRESPASSERS', *Steed looks up as it starts to hail.*
He puts up umbrella, heads for red phonebox.

> STEED
> I say, this is a bit much...

As he nears —

RED PHONEBOX

STEED *gets inside. Storm whips up, hammers against glass. Then*
hears RINGING. STEED *picks up* PHONE, *listens to —*

VOICE (V/O)
... Hello... Hello?... Who the hell...?
Who is this...? You have to get out
of the test area. I repeat leave the
area...

CLICK. *Line dead.* STEED *shelters 'Birds'-style, battered by raging storm, flying rocks. Bashing him against metal, hitting head.* STEED *blanks, concussion. Then —*

Storm dies. Mist clears. STEED *refocusses. Can't believe his eyes. Opens door, steps out into —*

DEEP SNOWDRIFTS

Sun on white snow. Same time, same place. But suddenly Steed seems to be in Arctic. Lone figure, white on white: thinks he's dreaming. Shivers. Picks up snow, powders thru fingers, as —

ON HORIZON

Figure moves towards him. Puff of snow on horizon. Like a mirage, zooooom! sled of huskies and ESKIMO *mushed to the max. Halts. Rider dismounts, from sled —*

A kinky boot in (fake) white fur.

Buckled straps. WOMAN *clad Inuit-Gaultier style in white fur catsuit: slit goggles, figure-hugging zipped cocoon.*

                              STEED
              Hello...

Slinky ESKIMO *vixen draws closer, goggles masking face. From sled, she takes out crossbow, aims, fires —*

HARPOON

Whhiinnng — thud!! Steed dodges as its jagged teeth rip into PHONEBOX *inches away. He takes stock, RUNS —*

Wading thru snow, pursued by ESKIMO *vixen. Who gains as* STEED *shivers in dead end, turns to face —*

Fur-clad Eskimo unveils goggles, REVEALING... 'EMMA PEEL'

> STEED
> Is that you, Mrs Peel...?

'EMMA' *moves in, eerie glint in eye. From zip, produces .38 gun, aims — Dirty Harry in slinky polar bear suit —*

> STEED
> Manners, Mrs Peel.

'EMMA's' POV: *'x' sights on his heart.* FIRES —

Blam! One shot — STEED *slumps into snow. Eyes close...*

FADE TO WHITE:

> EMMA (O.S.)
> Steed... Steed...?

FADE UP TO:

Steed's eyes blink open. Same landscape, no snow. Flickering glimpse of real EMMA *over him, very concerned.*

> EMMA
> What happened...?

Steed slips back into unconsciousness — Sound of CLACKING HEELS...

FADE OUT:

FADE IN:

INT. EMMA'S APARTMENT — DAY

Steed comes round slowly. Strange bed. Strange ultra-modern bedroom. Hears click-clacking of heels. Double take as he sees —

EMMA *deliver tea to his bedside, next to fruit bowl.*

>   EMMA
>   Tea... with lemon.
>   *(Emma picks a grape)*
>   Grape...?
>   *(Steed shakes his head)*
>   I bought them specially. Mind the
>   pips...

No reaction from Steed — still dubious. Emma shrugs. LONG REACTION SHOT as Emma walks downstairs, over to piano, chattering. Curious, Steed gets up, looks around.

>   EMMA
>   I hope you don't mind me taking
>   liberties. I had to tuck you up in
>   bed. You didn't seem in good shape
>   when I found you...

Steed peers down, as Emma plays cool Bach piano.

>   STEED
>   I was frozen stiff. Now I feel much
>   revived.

>   EMMA
>   Not me you should thank for that.

>   STEED
>   Actually I wasn't about to. I recall a
>   very strange thing. You tried to
>   shoot me, didn't you?

EMMA
How absurd. I would never shoot
you, not without my reasons.

STEED
I remember it clearly. One shot to
the heart. Luckily...
 (Removing bullet)
... my Trubshaw waistcoat was
bulletproof.

EMMA
Silly me. I thought you were just
overdressed. 'Be prepared': is that
your motto?

STEED
I thought it best to take precautions.
One never knows.

EMMA
I suppose Mother warned you
about women like me —

STEED
Until now, I didn't think there were
women like you —

EMMA
Obviously. I'm the sort that doesn't
take 'no' for an answer —

STEED
I think that would depend on the
question, Mrs Peel — I say, you are
definitely Mrs Peel, aren't you?

EMMA
You're delirious. I should have
abandoned you. Nursing an invalid

isn't my idea of fun after all. I could
have taken up any amount of
offers —

                    STEED
And?

                    EMMA
I did find a clue at Sir August's. You
see, Steed...
            (Beat; Steed curious)
A woman's touch.

*Impressed, Steed watches Emma's hands glide expertly over
keyboard. She moves away, keys continue automatically —*

As EMMA *shows* STEED *a toy snow-shaker. On its underneath: 'The
Wonderland Weather Corporation'...*

                    STEED
                (Reading)
Wonderland Weather...

EXT./INT. WONDERLAND WEATHER — DAY

CLOSE UP:

finger on buzzer. Door opens, revealing —

STEED *and* EMMA *inside reception area, like high-class jeweller's.
On walls, big pictures of clouds, rain, sun. At receptionist's desk,
snooty young Sloane,* TAMARA.

Steed pours on charm, much to Emma's annoyance.

                    STEED
        Hello... Wonderland Weather?

TAMARA
Yes. Can I help you?

STEED
Do hope so. We've been recommended by a friend who said you'd
know all about our problem. We're
awfully worried about our roses...

TAMARA
I don't understand.

STEED
My colleague and I represent
FLORA — Flower Lovers Of Ross-&-
Cromarty Association — a very
influential group of flower growers
working under tremendously
adverse conditions. For some years
we've been breeding a special rose,
the Crimson Monk, until in the
past week we've been plagued by
ladybirds.

TAMARA
I thought ladybirds loved roses —

STEED
A little too much. Now our flower
show's coming up, we need a few
more warm summer days very
quickly —

TAMARA
I don't see how I can help.

STEED
You don't? Have you seen a seven-
spotted ladybird in the mating
season? Speckled grey larvae. A

month to pupate, then — no more
roses. Voracious...
>   *(Steed moves closer)*
I hope I haven't come to the wrong
place. I was recommended by a
member of BROLLY.

>   TAMARA
> BROLLY?

>   STEED
> Don't say you haven't heard of it. I
> was speaking to my colleague Sir
> August — you do know Sir August
> De Wynter...?

>   TAMARA
> Of course.

*Emma looks up from copy of 'Cloud Seeding Weekly', Tamara leads
Steed and Emma thru back door into —*

INT. WONDERLAND WEATHER — SHOWROOM — DAY

*Dimly-lit in burgundy velvet with glowing spheres, large fish-bowl
size, at eye-level. On wall, pictures of Turner and Constable skies.
Tamara leads Steed and Emma —*

*Over to see inside — tiny 'MICRO-WEATHER SYSTEMS' of sun,
snow, rain: full of clouds and gases, as if alive:*

>   TAMARA
> Our newest line. Summer or winter,
> Tuscany or Gstaad. Natural
> weather delivered down your
> phoneline. All you'll need is a radio
> transmitter —

STEED
How real will it feel?

TAMARA
Very. A whole new line in
personalised meteorology. Imagine.
An autumn mist, dappled sunshine
through an orchard glade,
temperature...

STEED
Around 65...?

TAMARA
Whatever you fancy, sir.

STEED
Sounds marvellous. A solution to
matters meteorological and
horticultural. And to my roses —

As STEED *charms* TAMARA, EMMA *snoops. Sees slogans: 'Be natural.*
Act natural. Think natural. The natural beauty of Wonderland
Weather.' Intrigued by a model on ad LIKE EMMA. *As phone rings —*

TAMARA
One moment. Excuse me...

STEED
Hurry back.

By now putty in his hands, Tamara exits. Steed jams door, heads for
other door marked: 'STAFF ONLY'.

Inside — corridor. Steed summons Emma, they move down corridor,
as —

VOICE (O.S.)
Gentlemen... today is history. The
world is watching...

INT. WONDERLAND OFFICES — DAY

A sleek boardroom. A big TABLE. *Around it in chairs —*

> VOICE (O.S.)
> ... Together, we can make our world
> more wonderful. For you. For me.
> For mankind. Because now,
> Wonderland Weather warmly
> welcomes our new colleagues from
> BROLLY...

Eight TEDDY BEARS, *each six feet tall...*

Sinister, scary-looking. Bright pastel colors, furry, giant paws, ears. One sports a familiar tartan. Attended by two TEDDIES *in distinctive Red and Black costumes...*

The Tartan Teddy removes his head... REVEAL: SIR AUGUST. *Who circles table like a predator.*

> SIR AUGUST
> ... You all know who I am. And I
> know all of you. But you cannot
> know one another. Security is still
> paramount...

SIR AUGUST *moves round, pours drinks, a personal message for each* TEDDY. *Observing their body language for tell-tale signs:*

> SIR AUGUST
> ... Our organisation now faces its
> greatest test...

Dismay from Teddy Bears. Tension round the table.

> SIR AUGUST
> ... Therefore I must demand
> absolute loyalty, absolute
> obedience...

(He pours)
But anybody who wishes to resign
must do so now. And in recognition
of their work, a generous offer of
one million pounds awaits them...
(He waits)
Now...
(He looks round)
Does anybody wish to resign?
(No one raises their hands)
Please, don't be shy...

Down table, all TEDDIES *sit quietly. Each looking at the other. Meekly, one... then another* TEDDY *raise hands.*

SIR AUGUST *focusses on them. Magnanimous to a fault. Without missing a beat —*

SIR AUGUST
Ah, yes...
(He closes in)
We owe so much to both of you...
(Looks at TEDDIES*)*
Without your work, my humble
project would perish. How can I
show my appreciation?

Smiling benificently, from his brooch, SIR AUGUST *pops two lethal* DARTS *at* TEDDIES *— wham!! The two naughty* TEDDIES *slump over. Dead.*

SIR AUGUST
Any other business?
(Beat)
Now, let us all be upstanding...

SIR AUGUST *raises his glass, summoning* TEDDIES. *But no* TEDDY *dare remove costume to sip.*

SIR AUGUST
The toast is... absent friends.

INT. WONDERLAND OFFICES — DAY

Steed, Emma emerge into corridor. Left and right. Nothing coming. Head down hall. Up ahead —

Grand doors. They rush up, open doors, enter —

INT. WONDERLAND OFFICES — BOARDROOM — DAY

The boardroom. At table, Steed and Emma see two dead TEDDY BEARS. *Emma moves over, Steed inspects darts —*

STEED
Hm... A bullseye.

Emma leans forward, picks up a TEDDY's *head, mask falls off, revealing — a middle-aged* SCIENTIST.

EMMA
(Recognizing Teddy)
Babbington... Head of Prospero
Research...
(And other Teddy)
Morton, his assistant...

STEED
To lose one scientist is a
misfortune. To lose a couple —

More noise outside. Steed and Emma leave dead TEDDIES, *swiftly exit boardroom —*

INT. WONDERLAND OFFICES — CORRIDORS/ELEVATORS — DAY

Emma and Steed look down CORRIDOR *to see:*

BLACK TEDDY *dart across to stairwell, go* UP.
RED TEDDY *enters elevator.*

Action stations! Steed instantly leaps for —

STEED
Follow that bear — !

First elevator DOWN. PAN *with Emma as Steed's door closes.*

Camera moves to follow STEED DOWN, *as —*

EMMA *follows* BLACK TEDDY

INT. GLASS ELEVATOR — DAY

Inside glass elevator Steed travels DOWN — *looks across to* UP
elevator opposite, sees:

INSIDE GLASS ELEVATOR

Man-sized TARTAN TEDDY *glaring back at him —*

A cool doubletake from STEED, *watching* TARTAN TEDDY *woosh*
UPWARDS. STEED *looks back* DOWN, *sees —*

POV STEED: FROM DESCENDING ELEVATOR

a TRUCK *being lowered on automatic lift: beside it a strange*
SPHERE *transmitter —*

EXT. LOADING BAY — DAY

RED TEDDY *steps out of teddy bear uniform,* REVEAL: BAILEY...

Nearby, DONOVAN *and other* BULLY BOYS *load* SPHERE *into truck.*

EXT. ELEVATOR WALKWAY — DAY

STEED *steps out of elevator.*

EXT. LOADING BAY AREA — DAY

STEED *enters loading bay. Sees* BAILEY, DONOVAN *and* BULLY BOYS *loading sphere.*

They turn. STEED *advances.*

> STEED
> I say...

BAILEY, DONOVAN, *and* BULLY BOYS *run up,* STEED *in f.g., waiting. About to go for him,* BAILEY *taunts —*

> BAILEY
> A tailor's dummy. Look at that hat...

BAILEY *and* BULLY BOYS *head towards Steed, as —*

> STEED
> I wouldn't if I were you.

> BAILEY
> Well, I never. It talks.

CUT TO —

EMMA'S POV

of BLACK TEDDY *going up staircase.*

CUT TO —

CLOSE UP *of* EMMA *as she scans maze of staircases. Sees shadow.*
Chases after it. Low angle CLOSE UP *of* BLACK TEDDY, <u>*slowly*</u> *turns,*
looks down at EMMA —

CUT TO —

INT. LOADING BAY — DAY

On cue BAILEY *and his strongarm merchants attack —*

BAILEY *suddenly hoists* ARM *round Steed's throat,* DONOVAN *grabs*
Steed's arms. BOY #3 *lifts off his* BOWLER, *tries it on.* BOY #4 *takes*
aim with his fist, as suddenly —

BAILEY

Try this for size —

STEED *ducks,* BAILEY *takes the punch —*

WHAMMMM — *! Steed coolly elbows* BAILEY *in stomach — who*
slumps against wall. Slammm — ! kicks his Trubshaw hand-made
shoe into DONOVAN's *gut, and — swivels round to — Urrghhh !! —*
chop to THROAT *of* BOY #3 — BOY #4 —

Who slumps to floor. Steed catches flying bowler, in a fluid move-
ment, swivels round, kerrracckk — !! Smashes bowler into BOY #2's
face, stopping him dead. Around him four BULLY BOYS *on*
ground —

Recovering from punch, BAILEY *slips away to truck —*

CLOSE UP: *Steed replaces bowler, sees —*

POV STEED:

Revving engine, from truck BAILEY *drops paper map, it flies out of*
window —

Steed walks into his own POV, *moves toward* —

As BAILEY *guns* TRUCK *engine*, STEED *snatches map, as* —

> STEED
> Tsk, tsk. Careless boy —

Vrooom — *!* TRUCK *zooms off* —

EXT. WONDERLAND ROOFTOPS — DAY

HIGH ANGLE

of BLACK TEDDY *running from spiral staircase.*

TILT UP

To top of staircase, as EMMA *appears. Who runs down spiral staircase* —

TILT DOWN

With Emma to PICK UP...

BLACK TEDDY *running towards camera* —

POV BLACK TEDDY:

EMMA *running towards* —

EXT. WONDERLAND ROOFTOPS — DAY

The TEDDY *disappears thru an upstairs door. Which slams as Emma follows, until as she opens door* —

EXT. WONDERLAND ROOFTOPS — DAY

Emma follows like a cat, stalking a figure... Now you see her, now you don't, until —

Sudden flash — EMMA *sees* TEDDY *dart out —* EMMA *pursues, closes —* TEDDY *rushes on towards —*

EXT. WONDERLAND ROOFTOPS — DAY

EMMA *looks. Rooftop maze over city. She starts to search roof — turns corner to see —*

Sudden drop to streets, several floors below. Twinge of vertigo. As EMMA *stands alone —*

AGAINST SKYLINE

poised for action: Emma's ears listen out for noise... A bird's wing. Hum of wind, then... Emma senses...

From behind, a noise. Emma freezes — tense. Another NOISE, *Emma swivels round, as from —*

BEHIND PILLAR

Wooomphhhh!! BLACK TEDDY *attacks — swift volley of blows —* EMMA *reels back, loses balance — on her back*

OVER LEDGE

BLACK TEDDY POUNCES *on* EMMA. *Pins her down. A surreal moment of*

EMMA *suspended over ledge, grappling fierce* TEDDY BEAR *with murderous intent —* EMMA *parries, counter-attacks,* CHOP *to* TEDDY's *neck — she makes* CONTACT —

BLACK TEDDY's *head goes flying off! Revealing, to Emma's amazement...*

Another EMMA.

Wow. Her face. Eyes. Look. An identical double — call her BAD EMMA: *eyes flash — eerie* GLINT —

> EMMA
> Well, well...

A crazy MOMENT *— eye contact between* EMMA *and* BAD EMMA *— like twisted mirror locked in lethal embrace, as —*

ONTO ROOF

Emerges STEED *from stairs. He shouts —*

> STEED
> Mrs Peel — ?!

To his amazement in a slow reveal, Steed sees...

Two EMMAS. *Stunned, Steed moves towards, but* BAD EMMA

LEAPS

like a scalded cat, PUSHING PAST *him, and —*

Jumps clear!! Hangs in air, pushes out for edge. Lands, vanishes into rooftops. Steed pulls EMMA *up from ledge.*

> EMMA
> Glad you're here. Just in time to
> save me from myself.

> STEED
> I thought I was seeing double.

EMMA

We both were.

INT. BUS — NIGHT

Upstairs, windows blacked out: temporary HQ. BUS *drives thru streets.* STEED *seated,* MOTHER *tries to control debriefing. Behind,* FATHER *in dark glasses.*

MOTHER

So now you're saying there are two
Mrs Peels?

FATHER

How preposterous.

MOTHER

Let me handle this, Father. I'm
in charge —

FATHER

So you keep saying.

As MOTHER *and* FATHER *start to bicker like a married couple,* STEED *reads his newspaper.*

MOTHER

You made your point about Mrs
Peel, very succinctly —

FATHER

We both know who's responsible.
This whole story's a red herring.
Quite impossible —

MOTHER

Nothing's impossible, Father. I
often think of six impossible
things before breakfast —

(Beat)
Thank you for your contribution.
If you'll kindly allow me to
continue —
(Beat)
Steed? As you were saying...

STEED *looks up from his newspaper.*

> STEED
> Someone's recruiting your Prospero
> scientists into a cover organization.
> But, not Mrs Peel —

> MOTHER
> If you're so sure she's innocent, do
> you have another suspect?

> STEED
> I may. What makes you so sure of
> an attack?

> MOTHER
> The World Council of Ministers
> meets on Saint Swithin's Day.
> Patron saint of...

> FATHER
> Weather...
> *(Beat)*
> You see?

> STEED
> That's what I've been trying to tell
> you. I saw both Mrs Peels. With my
> own eyes —

FATHER *can't resist the final word.*

FATHER
Personally, I always thought eyes
were much overrated.

MOTHER *presses bell. Bus stops.*

MOTHER
We can't waste any time. He has his
orders.
(To Steed)
Clock's ticking, Steed. I'm counting
on you.

EXT. BUS — NIGHT

*Steed descends stairs. Bus stops outside Emma's apartment.
Downstairs, Steed passes Brenda, in conductor's outfit.*

STEED
My stop. Keep the change...

Steed hops off, outside —

INT. EMMA'S APARTMENT — NIGHT

*Clock ticks, kettle boils. On floor, weather charts. Steed has his
BROLLY 'map'; studies chessboard, as Emma studies charts, nibbling
chocolate fingers.*

STEED
Mother and Father are convinced
an attack will take place. Could
someone like Sir August really
target a kind of weather bomb?
(Beat)
... Knight to Rook four.

EMMA

If they knew what they were doing.
It's all a question of protons and
ions —

STEED

Do explain.

EMMA

Left on their own, they repel each
other. Very unstable. Queen to
Knight six...
(Beat)
To achieve fusion they need a little
extra oomph.

STEED

A gentle embrace, rather than a
clinch?

EMMA

Low excitation energy, technically
speaking. Then... boom!

STEED

Ah... exactly.
(Beat)
Knight to Bishop five.

EMMA
(Points to map)
Look. I've been charting these
weather outbreaks. Queen to
Knight three... Check.
(Beat)
Are you paying attention —?

Emma examines maps with a pointer, which she swishes.

STEED
Absolutely. A believer in firm
discipline —

EMMA
Do you always obey orders?

STEED
Always. Except... when I don't.
Knight to Bishop four.
(Beat)
For example, if I were, perish the
thought, under orders to kill you...

EMMA
Pity you never told me.

STEED
Never asked. Can't mention
everything. We were getting along
so well.

EMMA
You didn't want to spoil the fun.

STEED
It would have put a damper on
things, don't you agree?

EMMA
I'm intrigued. Queen to Bishop
six...
(Beat)
What did you have in mind?
Nothing too messy, I hope.

STEED
No need to dwell on the unsavory
aspects. After all, according to your
file you're a psychopathic

personality with schizophrenic
delusions suffering from recurring
amnesia based on traumatic
repression leading to outbursts of
anti-social and violent behaviour.
> *(Beat)*

Knight to Bishop Four... check.

Steed moves chess piece, lets it sink in. Emma hurt.

> EMMA

Is that really what you think of me?

> STEED

Oh, well...
> *(Beat)*

Just my type, Mrs Peel.

> EMMA

Good. Because I think I've found
something.

> STEED

You never fail to surprise me.

> EMMA
> *(Pointing on map)*

On this map. A cluster of micro-
climates round a single area. Very
strange.

> STEED

'X' marks the spot.
> *(Beat)*

Your move.

Emma reaches over, moves her piece on chessboard.

> EMMA

Queen takes Knight. Checkmate.

OVER: *quiet thud of croquet balls, as —*

EXT. HALLUCINOGEN HALL — GROUNDS — DAY

In grounds nearby lake, SIR AUGUST *plays croquet against an opponent whose ball curves towards hoop.*

> SIR AUGUST
> Haven't I always taken care of you?
> We are partners, even though we've
> never seen eye to eye —

> FATHER
> *(Turns — looks into Sir August's face)*
> I can't hold off The Ministry much
> longer. This Mrs Peel, I'm warning
> you — don't let her get too close.

> SIR AUGUST
> *(Thru clenched teeth)*
> Good shot.
> *(While addressing his ball)*
> Mutton dressed as lamb...
> *(Hits his shot)*
> Don't worry. I'll take care of Mrs
> Peel.
> *(While walking up to her ball, stands on
> Father's ball; treading into ground)*
> You're playing rather well, Father!
> Shall we double the bet?

> FATHER
> Yes, I've never been able to refuse
> you!

FATHER *hits her ball up in air, misses.*

> SIR AUGUST
> Oh, dear... just missed. I win, again.

FATHER
I'm not sure you appreciate the
danger. They do say love is blind.

SIR AUGUST
(To himself)
That would make two of us...

SIR AUGUST *bangs her ball away towards a steep bank.*

SIR AUGUST
I think you'll stand a better chance
starting over there...

SIR AUGUST *sets* FATHER *off <u>towards</u> the edge. See* FATHER *head off wrong way, as* SIR AUGUST *walks on —*

HEAR OFF: *a loud crash.* SIR AUGUST *turns.*

SIR AUGUST
Mind how you go.

Screeeccchhhh — !! OVER *sound of motor revving, as —*

EXT. COUNTRY ROADS — DAY

Zooooommmm!! Emma's JAGUAR WHIZZES BY...

Vooommm!! Speeds thru country roads, round bends, over humpback bridge, round blind corner, then —

Wooooosshhh!!! accelerates towards us, as —

INT. JAG — DAY

Emma glances over, sees Steed shaken but not stirred.

> STEED
> I thought you lived on the edge,
> Mrs Peel. Is this as fast as you can
> go?

> EMMA
> Have I trespassed on a male
> prerogative?
> > *(Before his reply)*
> We're being followed.

Hears buzzing sound, Emma checks in mirror —

> STEED
> What's that noise...?

Steed turns, looks out rear window, as —

EXT. COUNTRYSIDE — DAY

Jag zooms down country road, as up in SKY *—*

Swarm of BEES *approach — fast — flying in,* REVEAL:

OVER CAR —

BEES *swoop overhead, deafening noise — swarm of giant mechanical killer* BEES *circle above, rotor blades whirring —*

Steed checks from rear window —

> STEED
> Insects. Bigger every year...

IN SKY —

above, BEES START ATTACK *blasting down at car —*

IN JAG —

EMMA

Hold on...

Emma takes evasive action. Extra ACCELERATION. *Zoooommmmm!!!*

IN SKY

BEES *fire cannons down at car*

ON GROUND

bullets RIP *up road, forcing our heroes' Jag to* TURN. *Engines roar,* BEES *pursue from sky, firing canons, narrowly missing car as Jag twists and turns —*

ON DISPLAY:

video shows railway bridge 'blip' ahead. As Jag zooms toward it, BEES *follow, trying to catch up, as ahead —*

LOW BRIDGE

Emma drives thru, BEES *try to follow Jag under bridge, but splatttt!! Some* BEES *smash into* WALL. *Emma revs engine, pushing thru other side, as —*

BEES *zoom thru bridge, closing in hot pursuit —*

ON DISPLAY:

number counter goes down, meanwhile...

IN MINI

BAILEY *lies in wait, as...*

IN JAG

rear window is shot thru to REVEAL: BEES *zero in on attack. Emma*

glances, Steed turns, SEES — BEE *accelerating towards them...*

Emma looks up ahead, reacts as —

POV EMMA: *sharp corner dead ahead —*

She brakes...

Jag slows...

BEE *doesn't. And...*

Kerrrrassshhh—!! BEE *crashes thru Jag's rear window, forcing Steed to finish the* BEE *off...*

ON DISPLAY:

number counter decreases by one

IN MINI

up ahead — different angle — BAILEY *waits...*

IN JAG

Emma pushes foot down, Steed starts to strip gun from BEE...

OUTSIDE

Falling BOMBS *force Jag onto wooded track...*

IN JAG

Emma turns, following...

ON DISPLAY

map of wooded track...

IN MINI

BAILEY *and* DONOVAN, *waiting, as...*

IN JAG

Armed with bee GUN, *Steed starts shooting* UP *at attacking* BEES
overhead, bullets swishing past...
IN WOOD

*Jag speeds towards camera, dodging trees trying to shake attackers,
but* BEES *follow, tracking car in suicide mission as — splatttt!! one
or two* BEES *go* WIPE OUT *into trees—*

ON DISPLAY

new symbol indicates BAILEY *and* DONOVAN *lying in wait in
Mini...*

IN JAG

our heroes speed thru WOOD, *Steed fires from rear window.*

IN MINI

Pull FOCUS *from* DONOVAN *and* BAILEY *to... approaching Jag.*

IN WOOD

Jag zooms past Mini, pursued by BEES. MINI *gives chase...*

JAG *whips past camera...*

Followed by BEES...

Followed by MINI...

IN JAG

From rear window, Steed sees MINI *approaching...*

IN MINI

Bannnggg — !! DONOVAN *fires at Jag...*

IN JAG

Zinnggg — !! Bullets whizz past, Steed ducks back into car...

IN MINI

Blammm — !! DONOVAN *continues firing...*

IN JAG

Bannnggg — !! Steed returns fire then — Blammm — !! has to DUCK *to avoid* BEE *shooting from above. Under cover, Steed takes aim, and bannggg — !! fires up at attacking* BEE, *which —*

IN SKY

blammm — !! Hits BEE *dead on, which proceeds to...*

Fall to ground, onto its rotor BLADES, *which continue to* SPIN...

IN MINI

BAILEY *is about to shoot when...*

Up ahead, he sees crashed BEE *obstructing path, spinning and firing...*

DONOVAN *takes evasive action...*

MINI *swerves to avoid* BEE, *which...*

Still FIRES, *bullets exploding...*

DONOVAN *attempts to control car,* CRASHING *into forest...*

ON REMOTE CONTROL — BAILEY *loses control of* BEES...

ON DISPLAY — *bee 'blips' zoom round, as...*

IN FOREST — *Jag zooms thru, as* BEES *spin off in all directions...*

BEE-CAM *racing thru trees... zig-zagging until* —

Splattt — *!!* BEE *crashes* —

IN JAG

Emma and Steed thinks it's over. Until Steed turns...

IN MINI

Donovan and Bailey CRASH *out of the woods...*

Back onto ROAD...

Inside, Bailey REGAINS *control of the bees...*

IN JAG

Steed returns to seat, both Emma and Steed are startled by NOISE *on roof* — CUT TO:

ON ROOF

BEE *up on roof, shapes to* FIRE *its* STING —

IN JAG

Its STING *embeds itself into floor, just behind Emma and Steed...*

HOLD *as second* BEE *(rotor spinning) climbs thru in f.g....*

Bang — *!! Steed* SHOOTS *it, redirects* AIM, *and* —

Bannnggg — *!!* SHOOTS *roof* BEE...

Steed turns to face forward, reacts as...

BEES *swarm over front of car...*

Emma accelerates, turns wheel — mach force —

She swerves Jag from one side of road to other, SMASHING BEES *against trees or fence posts...*

As the Jag speeds away, one BEE *is left* HOVERING *over the petrol filler cap...*

CLOSE UP — *of* BEE, *as...*

It fires its sting...

Puncturing petrol tank. Fuel leaks onto the road...

From Jag, Steed SHOOTS *the* BEE...

The BEE *crashes into the petrol trail...*

And booom — !! IGNITES *it...*

As BEE-CAM *breasts an escarpment...*

REVEAL: *its* POV *of the Jag approaching a bend...*

IN JAG

Emma and Steed react, as up ahead they see —

POV — EMMA *and* STEED

The BEE *flying straight towards them, shooting up road ahead —*

REVERSE SHOT: *from* BEE, *rotors spinning, zeroing in on Jag —*

IN JAG

Emma shifts gear, accelerates...

Drives straight at the BEE...

Booom — !! BEE *bounces off front of Jag...*

Somersaults thru air, behind...

IN MINI

Bailey and Donovan react...

POV — BAILEY *and* DONOVAN: *of out-of-control* BEE *hurtling towards them, and...*

Kerrasshhh — !! Smashing into windscreen, as...

The Jag makes the corner, but...

The MINI *doesn't turn, and shoots* OVER *escarpment...*

IN MINI

Bailey and Donovan react, as...

POV — BAILEY *and* DONOVAN: *car rolls down embankment...*

Bailey and Donovan exit, as...

IN JAG

Emma and Steed react, as Emma drives...

Jag turning corner, trailing petrol...

BEND

Turns, skids, swivels round, suddenly —

POV EMMA:

An old lady (ALICE) *in road, directly in their path —*

Screeeeechh!!! Heavy braking, as Jag screeches to halt about half-an-inch away from her.

FROM JAG

As STEED *and* EMMA *get out,* BAILEY *and* BULLY BOY #1 (DONOVAN) *emerge with guns —*

> ALICE
> Would you please be so kind as to
> hit the ground — if it's not too
> much trouble?

POV EMMA: *sees to her surprise* ALICE *produce Tommy Gun, and —*

BANGBANGBANG — *!!* SPRAY BULLETS *into* DONOVAN, *who crumples, gun spinning along tarmac.* BAILEY *runs away —*

STEED *and* EMMA *react,* ALICE *unfazed.*

> ALICE
> I hope he was a baddy...
> *(Beat)*
> My name's Alice. Mother said you'd
> be on your way. This must be Mrs
> Peel.

> STEED
> Mrs Peel? Alice...

> EMMA
> How'd you do?

NOISE *as* DONOVAN *crawls to his gun, inches away.* ALICE *swivels — Bam! Bam! Two shots to the head.*

> ALICE
> Poor boy...

> *(Beat, then to Steed)*
> You with Mother or Father?

> STEED
> Both actually.

> ALICE
> Glad to see they're together at last.
> They don't get along. Promotion...
> Top job... Most unfair. Quite a fuss
> at The Ministry.

> STEED
> *(Not paying attention)*
> You don't say...

As STEED *and* EMMA *depart with* ALICE, *flames follow petrol trail towards car...*

> ALICE
> Someone didn't want you to get to
> the party.

> EMMA
> I expect we'll have to gatecrash.

> ALICE
> I may be able to help. This way...

BOOOOMMMM!! *Petrol tank explodes — !!*

Up ahead, wall-like battlements. Sign: NO TRESPASSERS. *Beyond, towers of Hallucinogen Hall. Steed surveys map.*

> ALICE
> Excuse me... you are a Gemini, Mrs
> Peel?

> EMMA
> How did you guess?

STEED
(Checking map)
There's Wonderland Weather.
Spot-on...

Up ahead murky, cloudy day. But sun shines over Hall.

EXT. HALLUCINOGEN HALL — MAZE — DAY

On lawn, PEACOCK flares tail — hidden cameras record Emma, Steed, Alice, inside walls. They move stealthily, unaware. Alice waves them on, entering into...

ALICE
Along here...

MAZE

Tall hedges surround Steed, Emma, Alice. They follow path, slopes, curves. Intrigued, then perplexed. Alice slips behind, Steed picks a rose, Emma rushes ahead.

EMMA
Aha... Yes... It's clear now. A love
maze in a trapezoid shape,
originally a late seventeenth
century design, then copied...

Steed sees Emma slip round corner. He pursues her. Glimpses her. On opposite sides of hedge.

EMMA
Over here. By your side.

STEED
I was worried...

At a hole in hedge, Emma sticks her face thru:

EMMA
How touching. Afraid you'd lost me.

STEED
No. That you might escape.

EMMA
Still suspicious?

STEED
Just wondering if you brought me
here under false pretences.

EMMA
Frankly, I'm amazed.
(Beat)
Perhaps I should run away.

STEED
I'll have to give chase...

EMMA
I'll hide — how romantic. Do try...

*She ducks. He loses her. Steed rounds corner — empty. He sets off in
search of Emma, meanwhile —*

Steed sets off, following BAD EMMA. *She disappears. He gives chase,
as —*

TWO EMMA PEELS

EMMA *swivels round. Sees* 'BAD EMMA' *behind her. Double take.
She disappears,* EMMA *gives chase —*

Round maze, EMMA *pursues* BAD EMMA, *following close behind.
Round corners... zig-zagging... sent wrong way... just missing...
until —*

EMMA *gaining on* BAD EMMA *double —*

She rushes onto a path strewn with leaves. As Emma steps over, she falls down trap — a giant rabbit hole.

INT. RABBIT HOLE

Down, down, down, Emma tumbles thru darkness, spinning helplessly like Alice in Wonderland... Corkscrewing head over heels, Emma ricochets from side to side —

> STEED (O.S.)
> Mrs Peel...?

EXT. MAZE — DAY

Steed turns a corner, oblivious to EMMA's *disappearance, sees* BAD EMMA *way down. She vanishes. He pursues. Until, he turns —*

Whammm!! A silver STAFF *whacks down,* STEED *finds himself staring face to face with —*

SIR AUGUST

> SIR AUGUST
> Sir August De Wynter.

> STEED
> John Steed.

Swisssshhh ! SIR AUGUST *swishes his* STAFF *— very fast, blurring —*

> SIR AUGUST
> An old trick I learned from a
> dervish in Istanbul...

SIR AUGUST *suddenly lunges at* STEED, *forcing him to move gingerly, parrying with umbrella —*

>STEED

Turkish rules?

Tic-tac-tic...

>SIR AUGUST

If you insist —

>STEED

Then try this —

STEED *gives* SIR AUGUST *a flurry of expert strokes, a match for Sir August's* LUNGES, *as he taunts —*

>SIR AUGUST

A man with an umbrella is a man
praying for rain —

Whack! SIR AUGUST *laughs, umbrella and staff locked together in a face off:* SIR AUGUST *and* STEED *close together —*

>STEED

And a man without one is a fool.
Never trust the weather, Sir
August —

>SIR AUGUST

Rain or shine...

Wooosh! SIR AUGUST *whacks* STEED's *umbrella away —*

>SIR AUGUST

... It's all mine.

POV STEED: *umbrella up in air, floats back down towards maze. Before* STEED *can respond —*

SIR AUGUST *vanishes into maze.* STEED *runs after him, swiftly loses him, then —*

STEED *turns corner, sees 'EMMA' running towards him.*

Too late, he realizes it's BAD EMMA, *who —*

Does a forward flip with a triple somersault flourish — swish — !
hands moving with 'virtual fighter' speed, until —

Whack! Punches him hard — lights go out. TO BLACK.

DISSOLVE THRU TO:

INT. HALLUCINOGEN HALL — INTERROGATION ROOM

A wavy, fuzzy screen slowly focusses. ABOVE *her...*

EMMA *awakes as if from a dream to see —*

SPIRAL HYPNODISC

that whirrs, creating trippy black and white zig-zag effects. Emma
lies helpless on special COUCH —

INSIDE GLASS CUBE

in mirrored Louis XIV style ballroom. From BEHIND *a familiar*
voice:

> SIR AUGUST (O.S.)
> So glad you could come.

EMMA *coolly looks down: straps across arms, legs.*

> EMMA
> Charmed, I'm sure.

INTO EMMA'S POV —

emerges SIR AUGUST *at his most charmingly diabolical. Dressed for*
romance, that twinkle in his eye.

SIR AUGUST
Comfortable?

EMMA
How cosy. Just the two of us.

SIR AUGUST
Like spoons in a drawer.

EMMA
Perhaps I could help you. If I knew
what you wanted...

SIR AUGUST
I only want one thing...
                    (Beat)
You.

EMMA
How touching.

SIR AUGUST
Join me, Emma. And we have the
world.

EMMA
You'd have to say 'please'.

SIR AUGUST
But, of course. If you insist...

*Sir August moves closer, coyly. Takes out wallet, selects a tiny poison
cupid's DART —*

*Wham! Aims and plunges dart into EMMA's heart — she jolts, poison
hits — SIR AUGUST cocks his head.*

SIR AUGUST
... Please?

He watches EMMA *go drowsy,* HYPNODISC *whirrs —*

ECU ON EMMA'S EYES

thousand REMS per sec — tiny chip transmits her unconscious images via wires onto her eyeballs...

> EMMA
> *(Blanking)*
> Your manners... leave much... to be
> desired...

SIR AUGUST *flicks* SWITCH.

IN MAZE

Steed is shaken awake. Eyes flicker open. Woozy, vision blurred, he sees Alice kneeling over him with some urgency —

> STEED
> I thought I was seeing double
> again.

> ALICE
> You were. A Gemini, definitely...
> *(Off Steed's look)*
> No time to lose. Here's the plan...

INT. HALLUCINOGEN HALL — ROOM

In full mindbending mode, spiral HYPNODISC *whirrs —*

SIR AUGUST

peers down over Emma, demented and lovelorn. He whispers intimately as she drifts off —

> SIR AUGUST
> *(Hypnotic voice)*

And when you awake, you will
remember nothing... remember
nothing... I, on the other hand, will
remember only ecstasy...

Emma struggles to resist, slips deeper into TRANCE.

> SIR AUGUST

Cloud...

> EMMA

... shroud.

> SIR AUGUST

Rain...

> EMMA

... pain.

> SIR AUGUST

Moon...

> EMMA

... June.

> SIR AUGUST

August...?

Emma pauses. Words won't come. SIR AUGUST *poised over her —*

> EMMA
> *(Like a nursery rhyme)*
> August is a lovely month, lovely as
> can be. First it loved poor Peter,
> now it's loving me...

> SIR AUGUST

Perfect. Perfect...

Sir August moves closer. He lowers lips... Closes eyes in

contemplation... Breathes in Emma's perfume, purses lips in tender...

KISS

Sir August moves back, misty-eyed... A finger to his LIPS, *tasting her... A sigh. Then...*

SIR AUGUST
Monsoon time...

INSERT: *gramophone needle drops down on vinyl. Sibelius's poignant 'Valse Triste' plays, as...*

FROM GLASS CUBE — EMMA *steps down in trance.*

SIR AUGUST *clasps her to him, hand on waist, enraptured, head spinning in a* SLOW WALTZ, *full of yearning and romance.* CAMERA *swirls round, as...*

SIR AUGUST *gazes deep into* EMMA'S *eyes, sweeping her* ROUND AND ROUND *until they float towards —*

A huge, ornate high-backed DIVAN. *He lays* EMMA *down, buries his head upon her breast. Slowly unzips catsuit, about to do the deed, when —*

In his EAR — RRRRIIINNNN—NNNNGGGGG!!!!!!

DOORBELL SOUNDS. *Loud. Repetitive. Unignorable.*

SIR AUGUST *tries to ignore it. But as music sticks the perfect moment is lost —*

SIR AUGUST *turns. On his face, a look: someone's going to pay for this...*

He heads for door, opens, then —

BANGG!!! SLAMS IT SHUT. *Noise echoes hard, rousing* EMMA. *Woozily she looks up, gets up shakily off divan, as —*

IN CORRIDORS

RRRRIIIINNNGGG!!! *Bell rings.* SIR AUGUST *thuds down corridors, heading towards front door, as —*

INTERCUT WITH —

IN CORRIDOR

POV EMMA

everything floats. She peers out, escapes down corridor, reeling, makes for door, as —

AT FRONT DOOR

RRRIIINNNGGGG!!! SIR AUGUST *opens to reveal —* ALICE *with charity worker's smile.*

> ALICE
> Raffle tickets, church fete. Poor
> Reverend Arbuthnot. His organ
> needs help. Perhaps a small
> donation...?

> SIR AUGUST
> No. Not today, thank you.

> ALICE
> Tombola, Lucky Dip, Pin-the-tail-
> on-the-donkey —

> SIR AUGUST
> Nor any other day.

Before Sir August can close the door —

> ALICE
> If you're going to be difficult, I'll
> have to insist —

From her handbag, ALICE *produces — a Magnum handgun.*

ALICE
Where's Mrs Peel?

SIR AUGUST *stares down the gunbarrel, as —*

OUTSIDE

STEED *darts thru maze of buildings. Heads for a window. Something odd. He taps 'window' — hard stone: painted fake. No entry —*

POV EMMA

everything floats.

DOWN CORRIDOR

Emma walks into room. Closes door. Down corridor, opens door. SAME room. She walks more... opens a door...

Again, uncannily EXACTLY SAME ROOM. Emma wonders if she's going out of her mind. Starts to run...

Down corridor. Opens door... the SAME. Uh-oh...

OUTSIDE

Steed roams ROUND. Moves towards back of house. Finds himself back where he started...

Steed moves towards wall of trompe d'oeil glass, starts tapping...

IN SITTING ROOM

POV BAILEY, *as he spies* ALICE *holding* SIR AUGUST *at bay, sneaks up behind her, cosh ready, raise it high and —*

Thwack!!!

BACK INSIDE

Emma hears NOISES... *a tapping, sinister laugh... shuffling feet... tinkling music box... Sir August's voice, repeating over and over... as*

Faster, Emma continuously spirals back on Escher stairs looping into SAME ROOM... *Like a fluttering bird, desperate to escape, Emma looks up.*

ON CEILING

classical motif, inspired by The Tempest — *four cherub Zephyrs blowing winds, four-pointed* COMPASS —

The tapping becomes louder, Emma pauses, a gamble. Emma scans all directions — heads... South.

Last gasp run towards wall MIRROR — *as if running towards herself, somersaults, leaps,* IN SLOW MOTION —

Kerrrasshh!! Crashes thru MIRROR, *splinters* SHATTERING — *mirrored* WINDOW *overlooking gardens, as she —*

EXT. HALLUCINOGEN HALL — WINDOW — DAY

Somersaults THRU *window down to ground.* THUD!! *Lands on wet ground. Looks up to see —*

Steed above her.

EMMA

Steed!

She struggles to feet, towards him, groggy, upset. Before a word — collapses in his arms in a FAINT.

INT. HALLUCINOGEN HALL — DAY

Inside hall of mirrors...

CLOSE UP: *Alone,* SIR AUGUST *winds up* TICK-TOCKING *clock, holds it to ear, soothing thwarted passion:*

> SIR AUGUST
> *(To himself)*
> '... My charms crack not, my spirits
> obey, and time
> Goes upright with his carriage...
> How's the day?'

But as he talks, from behind, shot of...

Sexily clad female lying on divan. CAMERA *rotates to* REVEAL: BAD EMMA *in scanty attire — black lace voile body stocking over hour-glass figure, irresistibly tempting, as —*

She speaks, open-mouthed like Coppelia doll:

> BAD EMMA
> *(Trying to mouth Emma's words)*
> Cumulus... Strato-cumulus...
> Nimbus...

She smiles. To no avail. SIR AUGUST *turns on* BAD EMMA

> SIR AUGUST
> I don't want you. I could make
> hundreds of you. Thousands.
> *(Shouts)*
> BRING HER BACK — !!!

Sulking, SIR AUGUST *storms out, hurls* CLOCK *at mirror which* SHATTERS. BAD EMMA *left all dressed up, her reflection in shards. He fills screen with* BLACK —

FADE UP TO:

INT. STEED'S RESIDENCE — SITTING ROOM — DAY

CLOSE UP — EMMA's *face. She wakes on day-bed inside Steed's elegant Regency-style residence: leather and mahogany, portraits, library in sumptuous style.*

Emma unsure of surroundings, Steed looms up.

>   STEED
> Don't worry. You're at my flat. Quite
> safe...

>   EMMA
> What am I doing here?

>   STEED
> Having tea.

>   EMMA
> Is that all?

>   STEED
> After a manner of speaking. Your
> boots...
>   *(Off Emma's look)*
> A delivery from Trubshaw's. They
> may come in useful. Allow me...

Steed presents pair of black leather knee boots, with fitted
MICRO-TAG. *Emma runs hands over.*

>   STEED
> I was worried. What happened to
> you...?

Steed kneels, helps her on with boots, brushing hands appreciatively over fine leather.

EMMA
I remember the maze, a house,
music, then... nothing.

STEED
Try to remember. It's very important.
Alice was onto something, and The
Ministry will want to find out.
You're in extreme danger. You
better stay here with me —

EMMA
Is that wise?

STEED
You'll be safer here. We can talk it
over. An official debriefing. With no
interruptions.

EMMA
You live alone?
(He nods)
No Mrs Steed?

STEED
Since you ask...

*Steed slides hand over Emma's boot. Taking his time before
answering, he moves closer to her.*

STEED
... Mrs Steed lives in Wiltshire.
(Beat)
My mother.

EMMA
I had you down as a creature of
habit. A bachelor's life.

STEED
It's worked quite well, until now.

EMMA
Don't tell me. You never met the
right girl.

STEED
There's always the exception —

EMMA
That proves the rule?

Steed's face now next to Emma's. Very close.

STEED
Quite. You're exceptional in many
things. But duty first. Shall we
make a start?

EMMA
A time and place for everything.

STEED
Now is definitely the time.

EMMA
And the place?

*Slowly, Steed draws closer to her. One hand on her boots. Feels
Emma's toes thru leather.*

EMMA
Too tight.

STEED
Push...

Faces close to one another, lips about to touch, when —

KNOCK-KNOCK!! *From hall, door flies open. Before Steed can move — from behind him, a familiar voice:*

>   FATHER (O.S.)
> Hello, Steed.

Steed swivels round, sees: FATHER *with* DR DARLING, *two Ministry* AGENTS *go to Emma —*

>   STEED
> It's normal for guests to knock.

AGENTS *hustle* EMMA *out.* FATHER *hushes* STEED.

>   FATHER
> We can dispense with formalities. I
> want Mrs Peel. Interrogation.

Behind Steed, appears Mother, pushed by Brenda.

>   MOTHER
> Nothing I can do about it, Steed.

>   FATHER
> Security restriction, Steed. You too.
> Mrs Peel is under arrest.

EXT. STEED'S RESIDENCE — MEWS — DAY

Moments later. Outside in cobblestoned mews, Emma bundled into a Ministry car. Father, Dr Darling and Agents look on, as —

Steed looks on. Emma glances back. A longing LOOK between Steed and Emma. Behind Steed, Brenda hovers.

>   BRENDA
> Sorry, Steed. Father's in control.
> Always wanted Mother off the case.

STEED
Only one place to go. I'll need
clearance.

BRENDA
I'll fix it. I can be very persuasive.
You only have to ask, John.
Whenever, wherever...

STEED
I'll keep that in mind.

Outside, Steed watches car ZOOM *off...*

DISSOLVE TO:

EXT. MINISTRY — DAY

High shot of MINISTRY, *somewhere by River Thames...*

INT. MINISTRY — BASEMENT CORRIDORS — DAY

*In tunnels, Steed strides down Ministry's murky basement corridors.
A Byzantine world of archive papers, part Lewis Carroll, part Kafka.
Knocks on door 'Room 282', Steed sees:* 'COLONEL I. JONES —
ARCHIVES'.

STEED
Hello-o...?

Steed pokes nose INSIDE. *A voice, from nowhere* —

VOICE (V/O)
Hello...?

STEED
Hello...?

VOICE (V/O)
Talk to the pipe. That usually helps.

CLOSE UP — PIPE PUFFING IN MID-AIR

WIDEN *to reveal: match lighting a pipe all by itself...*

INT. MINISTRY ANNEXE ARCHIVES — DAY

Inside archives, smoke belches from pipe, hanging in mid-air. Match thrown into an ashtray. Nobody there. Steed perplexed —

STEED
Colonel Jones — ?

INVISIBLE JONES (V/O)
... Don't worry about me being
invisible. Other than that I'm
perfectly normal.

STEED
I see.

INVISIBLE JONES (V/O)
Or rather, you don't. Learnt the
trick in camouflage. Till the
accident made a prang of things.
Tucked away in the bloody
basement now. Lucky if we even
get the tea trolley...

STEED
I don't have much time. I want you
to take a look at this map...
(Steed produces BROLLY map)
And I need to know more about the
Prospero Programme and
something called Gemini —

A chair swivels round. A drawer opens. A FILE *pops up, floats thru the air.*

>INVISIBLE JONES
>So you want to know about the
>Gemini Project... I have a digestive
>somewhere...

Biscuit, tea (spoon of sugar in mid-air) handed over.

>STEED
>This really is rather urgent, Colonel
>Jones.

>INVISIBLE JONES
>Call me 'Colonel' — no standing on
>ceremony.
>>*(Map lifted into air)*
>Hmm... Let's take a look...

Chair shifts back, Steed follows invisible steps. As Invisible Jones turns a corner, goes thru door into —

INT. MINISTRY ANNEXE ARCHIVES — DAY

Steed and Invisible Jones click-clack down corridor, one pair of SHOES, *two sets of* FOOTSTEPS, *into —*

>INVISIBLE JONES
>The Gemini Project. Ah yes.

CORRIDOR

stuffed with filing cabinets like an Indian bureaucracy, files and papers, layered like geological strata. Thru doors, into

LIBRARY

where dust fogs Steed's view. Tall wooden shelves stretch up to ceiling: stuffed Top Secret boxes spill out with paper. Invisible Jones takes out torch.

>   INVISIBLE JONES
>   Happy hunting.

Undaunted, STEED *keeps one eye on ticking* CLOCK *as...*

INT. THE MINISTRY — HOSPITAL (PADDED CELL) — DAY

CLOSE UP ON *Emma's face.* POV EMMA: INTO FOCUS *behind glass, up in* GALLERY: FATHER *speaks thru intercom:*

>   FATHER
>   *(Filtered)*
>   Hello, Mrs Peel. Welcome back to
>   The Ministry...

WIDEN *to reveal Emma*

INSIDE PADDED CELL

of bright VINYL *in vivid color, bulbous and pneumatic. Emma realises she's in a (groovily sinister)...* TOP SECURITY INTERROGATION CELL.

UP IN GALLERY

Father stares at Emma in cell.

>   FATHER
>   ... Doctor Darling confirmed his
>   diagnosis. You're suffering from
>   delusions. An extreme psychotic
>   personality disorder. A classic
>   syndrome to overcome your
>   subconscious guilt... Would you
>   like to sit down?

EMMA
I'm fine hanging around.

FATHER
We need to talk.

EMMA
About the weather? How topical.

FATHER
It'll help pass the time.

Emma starts to talk rapidly, as if forcing herself to recover her reason. Ends in half-gabble, half-sense...

EMMA
Time would pass anyway, if you
think about it logically. But then, so
few do think logically, or even
anti-logically. Clockwise or anti-
clockwise, tick-tock tock-tick, see-
saw margery daw, it amounts to the
same thing. After all, how do you
know I'm the real Mrs Peel — ?

FATHER
How real do you feel, Mrs Peel?

Father grins. Emma accelerates her insane logic —

EMMA
I'll repeat the question, bypassing
the weather — which no doubt
being British, we'll return to in a
moment. Do I walk like Mrs Peel,
talk like Mrs Peel? Am I witty, wise,
wonderful to know? Or do I go
round shooting Ministry agents
and attempting to rule the world
on my days off? No doubt about it,

logically or even anti-logically, by
definition, whatever the weather,
I'm going mad —

FATHER
Now you're playing games —

*Emma snaps out of it. A cold stare up at Father. In distance, chimes
of* BIG BEN *ring out, as —*

IN GALLERY

Father presses a button, disappears.

IN CELL

Emma waits. DOOR *to cell opens. In walks...* FATHER.

As Emma turns, beside Father she sees... REVEAL :

BAD EMMA

Looking straight at EMMA. *Very hostile.*

Before EMMA *can say a word — Father produces a gas canister,
and —*

Psssssssttt!! gas hisses out, EMMA *slumps unconscious,* PICTURE
blurs dreamily, FADING OUT...

EXT. SERPENTINE — ANGLES — DAY/DUSK

Bully boys place transmitter... A dial turns. Beep-beep... a flashing
LIGHT *says 'transmitter* ON'...

*Which connects with a transmitter... hidden among trees (on
Serpentine Island) which* BEEPS!!

The Serpentine radio TRANSMITTER *is...* ON!!

INT. MINISTRY — ARCHIVES — DAY

Focus sharpens with projector LENS *as — On wall, archive slides projected on Gemini and Prospero...*

Several cups of tea later, Steed is onto something:

CLOSE UP: *pic of smiling* SIR AUGUST *with* 'DOLLY' *and* 'DOLLY', *two cloned sheep. Steed flicks thru pages of Gemini Twins (human anatomy + bio-circuitry) as* INVISIBLE JONES *passes files —*

> STEED
> Gemini... Gemini... Of course... A
> Ministry cloning experiment. Sir
> August ran it but it appears he
> went too far. They pulled him off...

> INVISIBLE JONES
> But Sir August was under Ministry
> surveillance after Gemini.

A file whisks thru air, passed to Steed. On wall: slides of younger Sir August with Father; Gemini and Prospero plans; location sites (inc. Serpentine)...

> STEED
> Surveillance — by Father?

> INVISIBLE JONES
> Yes. Sir August could only set up
> Prospero after Father gave him an
> 'all clear'. So Mrs Peel never knew...

> STEED
> I see. So when Mother took over at
> The Ministry, Sir August joined
> forces with Father —

> INVISIBLE JONES
> Eeny-meeny-miny-mole... Bingo.

INVISIBLE JONES *blows smoke ring in air, moves in front of projector beam: light sculpts bodyshape in* 3D.

> STEED
> It's all in here. Why didn't you ever
> tell anyone?

> INVISIBLE JONES
> Nobody ever asked...

Invisible Jones blows smoke up to a glass grate in ceiling covered in SNOW. *Steed looks up* —

> STEED
> Is it my imagination — or is it
> getting colder in here?

EXT. LONDON STREETS — VARIOUS ANGLES — DAY/DUSK

The city evacuated, like war time... Deserted streets... lines of empty taxis... A sense of unease and urgency in ominous signs...

A sudden WIND *licks up, blowing paper down streets... The leaves on trees flutter... A weather vane turns...*

On WATER... *the Serpentine lake ruffles its surface, as...*

CLOUDS *move quickly past, casting shadows on ground... Swarms of birds zig-zag thru sky, emigrating in summer, as everything is empty... A beautiful church... Closed shops... as...*

EXT./INT. MINISTRY — 'HALL' — DAY

Inside grand hall, the 'WORLD COUNCIL OF MINISTERS' — *a global super-UN group — is in session round enormous tables. At far end, ornamental* GLOBE. *Tempers fray, ties undone, heated argument between Doves and Hawks* —

> HAWK MINISTER #1
>
> ... These changes in weather are
> controlled and aggressive. We have
> to respond with force —

> DOVE MINISTER #1
>
> You disregard the fact we came
> here to inaugurate a defense
> treaty —

> HAWK MINISTER # 2
>
> And you disregard the fact these
> secret tests are already hostile —

> DOVE MINISTER # 1
>
> I've said repeatedly —

> SIR AUGUST (O.S.)
>
> Enough — !!

Bam!! A STAFF *is slammed on table for attention.*

Out of SHADOW, *in explosive entrance,* SIR AUGUST *walks over to* MINISTERS, *pointing with his* STAFF —

> SIR AUGUST
>
> ... Now is the winter of your
> discontent...
>> *(Beat; points)*
> ... Above you, the weather is
> changing. The temperature is
> dropping...

Open-mouthed in shock, a MINISTER *breathes out — his visible breath hangs in mid-air.*

> SIR AUGUST
>
> ... Soon it will be freezing...

With his staff, SIR AUGUST *snaps* MINISTER's *mouth shut.*

SIR AUGUST
Why...? Hmmm...? Why...?

He looks round for an answer. None comes. He decides to let them in on his secret.

SIR AUGUST
The weather is no longer in God's
hands...
(Can't suppress a smile)
But in mine.

MINISTERS *shout out 'Impossible!' etc. But* SIR AUGUST *talks over them, strides down —*

SIR AUGUST
(Continuing)
Those clouds...
(Pointing with staff)
All controlled by me... Are
recreating the weather.
(Murmurs; shouts)
I have set off a chain reaction that
will paralyze and ultimately destroy
the city. The countdown has
already begun. And this is merely
the beginning—

Uproar as MINISTERS *shout:* 'Blackmail!' 'Outrage!' 'Get him out!' 'Crazy!' 'Unacceptable!'

SIR AUGUST
(Uproar; he raises staff)
Oh, do shut up —

SIR AUGUST *calms* MINISTERS, *conducting like an orchestra.*

SIR AUGUST
... Hundreds of millions will die.
They will freeze, drown, burn. With
ice, snow, sun, rain, all under my
control...
(Smile)
You and your governments have no
choice. You will buy your weather
from me. And, by God...
(Not joking)
... You'll pay for it.

MINISTERS *shout out rejection —*

HAWK MINISTER #1
This is unacceptable —

HAWK MINISTER #2
We won't yield to a madman —

SIR AUGUST
As you wish...

As he talks, SIR AUGUST *has crossed room, ready to exit. He stands over the ornamental* GLOBE *like a golf ball, steadying* STAFF *like a club —*

SIR AUGUST
(Practising his swing)
Enjoy it while you can...
(Smile)
Oh, by the way... You have until
midnight... tonight.

A smooth BACKSWING — *whack!!* SIR AUGUST *hits the* GLOBE, *which — ping! — rockets past gobsmacked faces of* MINISTERS. *Doors* SLAM!!, *as —*

INT. MINISTRY — CORRIDORS — DAY

Urgent sound of footsteps, as Steed races down Invisible Jones corridors —

INT. MINISTRY — PSY OPS HOSPITAL (CELL)

At cell door, CLICK *— a seal is broken.* STEED *rushes in, looking for* EMMA. *Finds inside the cell...*

Nothing. CLOSE UP: STEED *— new resolve. On his watch,* STEED *coolly presses a button —*

Beep-beep-beep... On Emma's trail.

INT. MINISTRY — CORRIDORS — DAY

CLOSE UP: *on* EMMA's MICRO-TAG *inside her Trubshaw boots. Beep-beep tag sounds subliminally, as...*

Up a corridor, FATHER *leads the way as* BAD EMMA *cradles groggy* EMMA *in her arms. On Emma's boot,* MICRO-TAG *beeps,* POV EMMA: *hazy vision of* BAD EMMA *above...*

DOWN CORRIDORS

Father strides on, BAD EMMA *and* EMMA *behind...*

INTERCUT

STEED *racing up corridors towards them...*

IN LONG MINISTRY CORRIDOR

FATHER *reaches exit with* BAD EMMA *and* EMMA. *When...*
A side door opens, REVEAL:

MOTHER (O.S.)
Sorry, Father. The game's up...

AT DOOR

Father turns to 'see' Mother, pointing a tiny revolver at her. Full of scorn, Father lets it all come out.

FATHER
(Re: gun)
Careful with that. Might go off.
Wouldn't want another accident,
would we? Only half working, as
you are...
(Walks towards)
Poor Mother. You finally figured it
out — too late.

MOTHER
Nonsense. Mother knows best. I
want you to release Mrs Peel.

FATHER
Certainly. But which one?

Mother looks at one... then other. Hesitates, and —

*Father makes her move: STRIKES Mother — gun knocked away —
Mother retaliates — struggle — until Father PUSHES Mother over —
sends chair circling round on automatic — Father ESCAPES —*

FATHER
It's really not Mother's day...

BAD EMMA *follows with* EMMA. *Father exits.*

EXT. HOUSES OF PARLIAMENT

Blizzard escalates.

INT. MINISTRY — 'HALL' — DUSK

Inside the hall — the MINISTERS *are locked in — Outside blizzard falls. They rush to look out of window. Ulp! Open mouthed reactions, as —*

> HAWK MINISTER #1
> Oh, my God...

The MINISTERS *look out, realizing...*

Big mistake.

EXT. MINISTRY — DUSK

Outside, blizzard raging, SIR AUGUST *settles back inside streamlined Rolls,* BAILEY *ready to drive. On front of car...*

PULL BACK, REVEAL: *giant snow plough.*

INT. MINISTRY — CORRIDORS — NIGHT

Alarm still sounding... STEED *racing up, finds injured* MOTHER —

> MOTHER
> The roof, Steed... the roof — !!

Steed races out, onto —

EXT./INT. MINISTRY ROOF — NIGHT

Steed emerges into night air. Blizzard rages.

STEED
My God...

IN DISTANCE — *across a* WIDE GAP — *he sees —*

EXT. MINISTRY ROOFTOP — NIGHT

Amid blizzard... looming from FOG, *vast onion-like shape, silk sides billowing like Jules Verne monster. Gas cells, liquid oxygen: souped up hi-tech meteorological* BALLOON...

Inside cockpit, FATHER, *ready to escape.*

                      FATHER
          Better luck next time, Steed.

STEED *races over to edge, no exit — immediately dodges down a fire-escape, heading for street level, as —*

ON ROOF

from another entrance emerges BAD EMMA, *still cradling* EMMA *in her arms. As* EMMA *hits the open air, she* REVIVES, *sees* BALLOON *up ahead, flames from its liquid oxygen tank, and —*

BAD EMMA

towering above her. As BAD EMMA *walks her out to the balloon,* EMMA *seizes her chance,* SWIVELS *round and —*

Chop!!! Karate chop to neck of BAD EMMA, *who* DROPS EMMA *down.* EMMA *regains balance, watches* BAD EMMA *reel round, want* REVENGE — AIM *for her with rapid* FLIP —

KICK

Ooooff!!! — impact hits EMMA *backwards, dangerously* CLOSE *to edge.* BAD EMMA *is onto* EMMA *in a flash,* HOLDING *her over edge as*

IN BALLOON

FATHER *starts to coil up* LADDER *into balloon. With a* LEVER *and* NOZZLE *she releases* GAS, *boosts* FLAMES *which fill helium balloon, hot air cone billowing wildly —*

EMMA

close to panic, until gasping for breath, she KICKS BAD EMMA *off, sending her hurtling onto roof. But* BAD EMMA *is only a...*

MACHINE. *She gets up... really mad...*

EYES

glinting... and ACCELERATES *towards* EMMA *who —* CRUNCH *of* BONE *on* BONE *— tries to dodge and parry* KICKS, *until* BAD EMMA *seizes* EMMA *in lethal —*

EMBRACE

grabs hold of EMMA, *leaps up to* GRAB *hold of* LADDER

FROM BELOW

STEED *down at street level looks up thru buildings at distorted angle, to see up in* SKY:

POV STEED — LADDER *coils up, with* TWO *tiny* EMMAS *dangling down from it over a sheer drop.*

ON STEED *— as —*

BALLOON *starts to drift over city, Steed follows, as —*

TOWARDS CAPSULE

BAD EMMA *hoists* EMMA *up, straining over last few feet — onto* TOP, *where flames are blazing, they* FIGHT —

BAD EMMA *pounces. Caught in vice-like grip,* EMMA *tries to fight back.* BAD EMMA *pulls* EMMA *to flames —*

Closer and closer...

EMMA *struggles frantically. Blindly,* EMMA *reaches for gas supply* LEVER, *with* HAND *grappling*

EMMA FLIPS LEVER, *which —*

WOOOOOOSSHHHH!!! *gas releases rapidly from tank —*

                    FATHER
          You fool...

ABOVE THEM — *the balloon quickly starts to* DEFLATE...

On nozzle: hissing gas...

CLOSE UP: 'LIQUID OXYGEN — DANGEROUS'...

On dial: arrow quivers off scale to 'DANGER'!!!

Emma watches BALLOON *lose height*

FROM BELOW

STEED *sees it deflate, lose direction and —*

ACCELERATE

into driving blizzard over fairy tale city, OK for a few hundred yards, until as it clears the rooftops, looming out of the fog, mist and driving snow is a HUGE

BILLBOARD

Its slogan... 'WONDERLAND WEATHER: SOONER THAN YOU THINK'... *They approach, get closer,* CLOSER, *until...*

FATHER *tries to throw* EMMA *over...*

>   FATHER
>   Throw her off...!

ON BILLBOARD

electrics SPARK *and* FIZZ *as balloon* LOOMS *closer, just before the balloon gets too close to the* BILLBOARD

EMMA IS THROWN OFF, *and —*

HURTLES DOWN INTO SPACE —

Behind her, BALLOON *slowly starts to* RISE. *Lifting slightly, as* BILLBOARD *closes, closer, closer, until...*

Too late. The Balloon can't make it —

CLOSE UPS: FATHER...

Even BAD EMMA...

Go ARRRGGHH!!

The balloon lurches into its doom, as —

Liquid oxygen + gas + max pressure + electrics + momentum =

BOOOOOOOOOOM!!!

BALLOON EXPLODES *in* HUGE FIREBALL —

FATHER *and* BAD EMMA *unable to escape — as* FIREBALL

WOOOOOSHHHH!!! *zips thru falling snow of blizzard —*

Against b.g. of fireball...

ON EMMA: *falling... limbs full stretch...*

ON STEED: *dread and horror...*

ON EMMA: *eyes wide...*

POV EMMA: *snow... blizzard... fog... ground looming up...*

ECU EMMA's EYES: *inside pupils — reflection of: a monument... statues... death staring her in the face...*

ON STEED: *eyes snap shut.*

BELOW

STEED *sets off immediately in pursuit of* EMMA, *as —*

EXT. LONDON ROOFTOPS — SKY — NIGHT

Over billboard, BALLOON WRECKAGE *hangs like a defeated monster, wires trailing —* SPARKS *still* SPLUTTER, ELECTRICS *spitting —*

Until... BOOOM!!

Like a FLASH *of fireworks, secondary* EXPLOSION *illuminates — slogan for* 'WONDERLAND WEATHER', *now dangerously* ALIVE!!!

EXT. LONDON STREETS — NIGHT

Blizzard rages...

Winds blow snow up to waist height. Shop windows submerged. Traffic lights beep green, no traffic. Down street, emerges

STEED

like Scott of the Antarctic in quest for Emma Peel. In hand, a beeping tag gives direction. Up front, overturned double-decker

BUS

Steed clambers over. Slides down. Up ahead...

Steed walks, turning into... an empty Trafalgar Square. Nelson's column shoots up. Lion statues.

Beeping accelerates. Emma close by... STEED *steps forward towards giant snowdrifts, where cradled in paws of a* LION STATUE *he sees a familiar figure —*

EMMA

Limbs outstretched, frozen in aspic, unconscious... Emma's eyes flicker. Alive and well, Emma smiles.

> EMMA
> Prince Charming, I presume...

Steed helps her up, carries her safely to ground.

> STEED
> Hardly. A micro-tag concealed in
> your boots, Mrs Peel...

> EMMA
> Thank you, Trubshaw...

Steed dusts her off, fussing over her.

> STEED
> How do you feel?

> EMMA
> No broken bones.

> STEED
> And the other Mrs Peel?

EMMA
Dispatched, I think. Sad in a way...

STEED
Hmm... I wonder...

Emma and Steed walk on, determined. But Steed looks puzzled at Emma. He can't get it out of his head. Is she, or isn't she? She picks up on his look, stops —

EMMA
Yes?

STEED
I can't quite get her out of my head.
I was just thinking...

Without warning, Steed suddenly pulls Emma towards him, KISSES her full on lips. As snow falls, Emma remains well and truly kissed.

Slowly, savoring it, until Steed pulls away.

EMMA
Unless I'm very much mistaken,
that was a kiss, Steed.

STEED
Yes... technically.

EMMA
'Technically'?

STEED
I would never presume. More in
the spirit of scientific enquiry. Hard
evidence, you might say.

EMMA
I realized that, immediately.

STEED
Of course, you did. I needed proof
you were really Mrs Peel.

EMMA
I see. And... convinced?

STEED
Still thinking...

EMMA
What are you thinking?

STEED
I need to keep a stiff upper lip.

*Steed and Emma set off thru blizzard, heading out of Square towards
Whitehall Ministry complex, as —*

EXT. TRAFALGAR SQUARE — SEVERAL ANGLES

Blizzard forms huge DRIFTS *of snow that start to* COVER *streets and
buildings. The city paralyzed, as —*

INT. MINISTRY — CONTROL ROOM

Back at controls, Mother on hotline to PM, Brenda tends fire.

MOTHER
(On phone)
Dense cloud formation moving
north east, sir. Some sort of radio
transmitter...
(Beat; listens)
Of course we have it under control,
sir...
(Beat; listens)
Well, not quite under control, but...

> (Beat; listens)
> Yes, sir. I understand sir. Our
> agents are on the case right now...
> > (Beat; listens)
> Two of them, sir.
> > (Beat; listens)
> A man... and a woman, sir.

INTERCUT WITH —

EXT. LONDON HOUSE — NIGHT

Close — thru a window a women shivers, closes curtain as we pull back thru deserted city streets, snow falls. Up over a building to reveal Serpentine Island.

EXT. ISLAND — NIGHT

Tall trees. Then beneath this fairy tale scene, just like a snow-shaker, two strange SHAPES move into view. At first, like white PODS, floating across water.

In misty haze of fog and tumbling snowflakes, they bubble and float ever CLOSER to the island. Perfect spheres, moving closer to the shore. As the...

PLASTIC BUBBLES

hit shore, REVEAL they are man-sized... CLOSE UP: immaculate surface perforates. Two slits appear. From inside, like human eggs, zips peel away to reveal —

STEED *and* EMMA

dandy in suit, bowler, umbrella, rose in lapel. She in leather gear. They land on shore, step out. Ahead, a jungle-like forest. Steed takes out his BROLLY map:

STEED
A walk in the park?

EMMA
How lovely.

STEED
An island in the Serpentine.
According to Colonel Jones, this is
a map of a secret Ministry
installation. Sold off years ago to...

EMMA
Wonderland Weather, I'd bet.

STEED
Quite.

Steed straightens lapels, Emma reminds him of the task.

EMMA
I think we should go. Do you mind?

STEED
Not at all, Mrs Peel.
              (Umbrella deflates ball)
... After you.

EMMA
No, after you.

EXT. ISLAND (SERPENTINE) — FOREST — NIGHT

*A jungle. Like explorers, Steed and Emma thread thru undergrowth.
Dark all round; among flitting shadows, CAMERA EYES of peacock
swivel towards them...*

Steed scents something suspicious. He ducks down —

EMMA
Something up ahead.

STEED
How are you with animals?

EMMA
Two-legged, or four-legged?

STEED
I wish I knew.

Steed and Emma sense SOMETHING *round corner. Emma parts branches to see, lying on ground, a six-foot tall —*

Pink TEDDY BEAR. *Dead.*

Emma and Steed rush over, Emma slips off its mask.

STEED
Alas, poor Teddy...

EMMA
I knew him, Steed.
(Beat)
Penrose... in charge of anti-matter
fission on Prospero...

STEED
The teddy bears must be having a
picnic. We're getting warm...

Steed and Emma push thru forest. Look up, frosty canopy of snow decorates trees. Suddenly, on ground —

Two more TEDDY BEARS *— Turquoise. Lilac. Dead.*

Emma huddles over furry corpses, lifting their masks as Steed goes on lookout. All round, forest shimmers. Wind thru trees makes strange harmonic sounds:

EMMA
(Checking TEDDY BEARS*)*
Professor Pemberton... and Dr
Nesbitt... Trail's getting very warm
indeed...

STEED
And warmer still, Mrs Peel. "Oh
brave new world, that has such
creatures on it..."

*Steed gets Emma to look further. Up ahead, Emma sees... a trail of
dead* TEDDY BEAR *corpses.*

EMMA
Hmmm... A little too warm.

Emma separates from Steed, goes to investigate trail: supine TEDDY
BEARS, *dead as dodos. Green. Scarlet. Mauve. Then...*

*Thru trees, Emma glimpses something, hears noise... Swivels round
to see —*

Ssssss! A razor-sharp pointed blade of silver STAFF *pointed at her
throat. Looks up to see* FROM MOONLIGHT *— Fresh from
teddy-bear cull,* SIR AUGUST.

SIR AUGUST
Sssshhh...
(Blade poised)
I could snuff you out in a
moment —

Unfazed, Emma taunts him, cool, defiant.

EMMA
Really? What a surprise. Always
trouble at a Teddy Bears' picnic —
I should have known.
(Beat)

Shall we dance?

                    SIR AUGUST
No. Not now. Too late for that —

                      EMMA
I thought you liked to dance —
how could you forget...?
"August was a lovely month, lovely
as can be.
Now it's turned to winter, cold as
cold can... — "

*Defiant, Emma tries to grab blade, swivels; swiftly Sir August blocks
her move, brings her eye to eye —*

                    SIR AUGUST
Foolish girl. Look —

A stray snowflake has fallen, SIR AUGUST *catches it.*

ECU*: snowflake crystal glimmering.*

                    SIR AUGUST
                (Re: snowflake)
So beautiful, so deadly. This
blizzard shall be your tomb. What
coffin could be more exquisite?
            (Blows snowflake at her)
Any final requests?

                    EMMA
Now that you ask, there was one
thing I wanted to clear up...

She looks. He knows, she knows. Taunting him.

                    SIR AUGUST
That...?

Furious, SIR AUGUST *presses his attack — razor-sharp point on Emma's cheek. She turns head away, his resolution wavers. A better idea: eternal torment.*

> SIR AUGUST
> Emma, dearest...
> *(Beat; laughs)*
> ... You'll never know.

Swwiiissshhh!! Emma swivels round — He's gone. Thru frosty mist, Emma turns to see —

> STEED (O.S.)
> *(Looming out of moonlight)*
> You're needed, Mrs Peel...

EXT. ISLAND (SERPENTINE) — PHONEBOX — NIGHT

RED PHONEBOX

Emma and Steed head towards phonebox, Emma enters.

INSIDE PHONEBOX

Steed squeezes in beside her. He reaches down, Emma eyes him, as she picks up the phone.

> STEED
> Excuse me. Equipment needs
> adjusting...

> EMMA
> Nothing broken?

> STEED
> *(Fiddles with)*
> My umbrella. Tight fit in here.

EMMA

Allow me...

(Into receiver)

'How now brown cow...?'

'The quick brown fox jumped over
the lazy dog' —

Emma presses 'Button B'. FLOOR LOWERS.

They both go down. HOLD, tilting down, into black.

INT. SERPENTINE — UNDERGROUND HQ

*Underground. A door opens. From darkness Steed and Emma
emerge, ready for action, into...*

*A bright empty white space, very low ceiling. No people, no alarms.
Nothing. Enigmatic and forbidding.*

Steed leads the way. They listen. Complete silence.

*Only tick-tack, tick-tack across floor. Exchanging wary glances, as
perspective changes, stepping into...*

*What appears to be an immense neo-classical parking lot, designed
by Robert Adam in a particularly sadistic mood: up ahead they see...*

PILLAR

*supporting a claustrophobic passageway. Tick-tack... shoes echoing
in the vast space. When suddenly —*

*Rinngggg-rinnnnggg!! PHONE rings. Noise startles Steed and Emma
who step round, looking for phone. Perspective changes, they see
whole ROW OF*

PILLARS

which carry on to vanishing point, low ceiling studded with immaculate Doric columns.

RIINNNNGG-RINNNNGG! *Steed and Emma search. Until* BEHIND
PILLAR, *old bakelite phone. Steed picks up.*

> STEED
> *(On phone)*
> Hello...? Hello...?

*Steed listens. Line goes dead. Emma watches Steed put down phone,
walk on. Casually —*

> STEED
> Wrong number.

*STEED and EMMA head off down vast promenade. Tick-tack,
tick-tack... echo in cavernous space. Until*

Ahead Steed and Emma glimpse what appears to be a

WINDOW

*gets bigger. Not one, but two... three... a whole structure of glass...
As they turn a corner, they see... a huge*

GLASS DOME

*Steed and Emma step up, look over. Can't quite see. Need to get closer.
They pause.*

> EMMA
> Should lead to the control module.
> Anti-matter circuits will be close by.

> STEED
> I wouldn't know where to start. You
> make it sound so simple.

> EMMA
> I did design it, after all.

Off Emma's superior look, Steed steps forward. Carefully, Steed and Emma set FOOT *on glass dome — tick-tack...*

WALK UP *the* DOME. *Until they look* DOWN *thru glass to* REVEAL HUNDREDS OF YARDS DOWN —

POV: STEED *and* EMMA —

INT. UNDERGROUND HQ — CONTROL ROOM

HUGE GLASS BUBBLE

as beginning, except this one's ten times as big...

A vertical TOWER. *A smaller* POD *(half way up) Steel catwalks connecting.*

AROUND VERTICAL TOWER

weather STORM *patterns* FIZZ *and* CRACKLE — *black* CLOUDS *spit rain — at* CENTRE *like a sea-borne oil rig:*

PROSPERO'S CAVE

REVERSE SHOT: *(from bottom of tower) of tiny 'X' shaped figures (Steed and Emma) spread-eagled on...*

GLASS DOME

Ulp! Steed and Emma peer down.

> STEED
> As you were saying, Mrs Peel.

> EMMA
> Hmm. A little bigger than I
> remember.

STEED
Anything else you'd care to mention
— strictly from the expert's
point of view?

EMMA
One thing. Soon the process will be
irreversible. We have a few minutes
before it blows.

STEED
How comforting. I'll stop Sir
August, you disarm the anti-matter
circuits —

EMMA
If I can find them.

Hisssssss!! A loud noise. From afar, a deep rumbling.

STEED
Your confidence is inspiring.

EMMA
Feeling's mutual. Shall we?

Tick-tack... Steed and Emma step off glass DOME. *They hear a slow
growl. Which grows. Floor starts to vibrate and hum, until...*

Roarrrrrrr!! Distant engine noise REVS *up! Electric current* HUMS,
until... Deafening ROAR *starts...*

Near pillar, Steed sees open staircase.

STEED
This way.

They head towards it, as the deep rumble grows, as...

CLOSE UP: *hand of* SIR AUGUST *as he* PRESSES *switch...*

INT. SERPENTINE HQ — UNDERGROUND CONTROL MODULE

Down in lower glass sphere, staff beside him, SIR AUGUST *sits, controlling storms.* ON MONITORS: BLIZZARD *sweeps city...*

> SIR AUGUST
> Anti-matter fission starts now. Five
> minutes and counting...

COUNTDOWN STARTS — *red numbers go backwards... In b.g., weather* STORM PATTERNS *fizz and* CRACKLE...

COMPUTERIZED VOICE STARTS TO COUNT... CLOCK TICKS.

EXT. SKY OVER LONDON — NIGHT

Moonlit night. On BIG BEN: *hands tick-tock away. In distance, dark clouds approach like an army, spreading shadows...*

EXT. CLOUDS

INSIDE CLOUDS — MOISTURE CRACKLES, *energy waiting to explode.*

EXT. UNDERGROUND HQ — WEATHER TUBE

Topshot from top of stairs

INT. UNDERGROUND HQ — WEATHER TUBE

Closing door behind, Steed and Emma clamber into vertical tower, down steps. On wall, Emma finds: old map detailing circuits layout —

Down tube... Steed and Emma see tight spiral stairs, into infinity...

Steed and Emma descend, HEAR *tremendous* NOISE...

All around, air charges with STATIC *electricity... Walls shake with engine* FORCE...

INSIDE TUBE *frost forms, colder by second, until...*

Inside, temperature plummets... Snowflakes fall as STEED *and* EMMA *descend... Fighting elements together. Storm increases until...*

> EMMA
> Must be a hatch somewhere. I need
> to locate the circuits, break the
> codes, disconnect the wires —

> STEED
> How will you know if it works?

> EMMA
> I won't — until I make the right
> connection. Better keep your head
> down —

> STEED
> So much for science. I'll stick to
> swordplay.

Now a roaring BLIZZARD *blows... Sudden micro-climate of* SNOW *and* ICE... STEED *and* EMMA *push on, slowly freezing... Valiantly persevering, until...*

Midway down, Emma finds what she's been looking for: a HATCH, *leading into junction tube. Emma turns a wheeled door —*

> EMMA
> This must be it — go down — don't
> wait for me —

> STEED
> Perish the thought...

(She turns; an afterthought)
Oh, just in case...

                    EMMA
... Good luck?

                    STEED
Something like that. Not that you
need it, of course.

                    EMMA
            (Beat; smile)
You might need it more than me.

A lingering look, Steed watches Emma exit thru hatch. Steed feels sudden breeze. Emma's door SLAMS shut, he looks down at what Emma meant. In distance:

A huge windstorm revving up, straight for him...

EXT. PARLIAMENT SQUARE — NIGHT

Near Big Ben's clock hands moving closer to zero hour, Serpentine radio TRANSMITTER bleeps against swirling Turner sky...

IN SKY

WHITE CLOUDS *darken into* BLACK, *billow with gases, gain mass as they roll thru* CITY STREETS, *turning into an airborne...*

INSIDE PROSPERO'S CAVE

SIR AUGUST *laughs, enjoying himself.*

                    SIR AUGUST
"Now does my project gather to a
head."
It's... TIME!

IN CITY — SEVERAL ANGLES

A beautiful violence WRECKS *the city... Beneath a violent sky in swirls of energy, a Blakean apocalypse of London... A double decker bus somersaults down a street smashing into a building. Windows explode, rooftops ripped off by hurricane winds.*

CLOSE UP — NUMBERS *fly...*

INT. UNDERGROUND HQ —

Blasstt!! hatch door opens, EMMA *crawls out, as metal grille falls into a windswept space —*

Emma grabs hold of platform, fingers coiling round, leaving herself HANGING *helpless over —*

VOID... *She looks down.*

> EMMA
> Uh-oh...

Vertiginous drop down towards GLASS BUBBLE. *In front, she sees other control module, a smaller...*

POD

attached to her tower wall by four angled steel RODS, *joists strain* CONTINUOUSLY *under weight, threatening to blow. Inside pod... a* CONTROL SYSTEM.

> EMMA
> Ah...

Poised on edge, as —

FROM INSIDE TOWER —

As STEED *continues down spiral stairs,*

UP THE TUBE *comes... A swirling ball of energy like an electric windstorm... Which* WOOSHES *up towards him, as it* HITS STEED —

Whhaaahammmm!

WIND BLOWS — *a sudden micro-hurricane picks him* UP... SLAMS STEED *against sides, flattened by 60mph* GUSTS *of* WIND. *As he loses grip, tumbles down —*

MUCH FURTHER DOWN, *Steed sees...*

A door. His only hope. A LONG WAY DOWN...

INTERCUT WITH:

Emma levers herself up, STEPS *on a rod... Which* CRACKLES *with energy, like a lightning rod —*

Emma has to set out across steel tightrope... Hand over hand, hanging over SHEER DROP *hundreds of feet down. Wire cuts into her hands...*

She pushes on... half way... POD *in sights... turns upside down, inches along towards* POD *as... From* ABOVE *Emma glimpses...*

BAILEY *crawling down angled* ROD *towards her.* RODS *start to* BEND *and* SWAY *in winds.* EMMA *inches onwards...*

BAILEY *gains, slipping then regaining balance...*

EMMA *inches across, closing on pod.* BAILEY *catches up. She pauses, lets* BAILEY *move* OVER, *then...*

DROPS *her foothold,* DANGLING *over* VOID...

Hands sweating: grip tight, losing power, as —

Ping!! One ROD *snaps like a whiplash, narrowly missing her...* BAILEY *drops down, heads towards* EMMA. *A few inches away...*

He moves as if to STAMP *on her hands...*

EMMA *flexes muscles, strength surges as she...*

LAUNCHES *into an acrobatic* FLIP *which...*

KICKS BAILEY *in stomach...*

Winding him, BAILEY *totters, as —*

EMMA *straddles over rod...*

BAILEY *tries to* PUNCH *and* KICK...

EMMA *gives a* CHOP *to his neck...*

BAILEY *swerves, loses balance, nearly tumbles, as —*

BAILEY *struggles to regain...*

Finally falters, TOPPLES *over,* DIVES, FALLING *into —*

VOID. *His yell disappears, echoing in distance...*

> EMMA
> Poor boy. No head for heights...

INT. UNDERGROUND HQ — 'POD'

Tossed by stormy winds, Emma regains balance, heads towards POD *its supports now weak, creaking and swaying. As lightning* FLASHES *down below —*

Emma throws switch —

WIDE SHOT *as the weather storms shut down. Temporary halt. Whole chamber quietens...*

Up in pod, Emma reacts. Sound of tick-tock. The pod creaks, starts to settle, as —

INT. UNDERGROUND HQ — TUBE

Inside the tube, weather storms have halted. Steed stops and listens. Eerie echoing silence. Hear his heartbeat...

A quiet, private moment. Very ominous, as —

INT. UNDERGROUND HQ — PROSPERO'S CAVE

SIR AUGUST *exits onto catwalk. Furious, he looks up. Worried, he scowls. Then an idea. Slowly, he smiles, turning into a...*

Devilish grin, as...

INT. UNDERGROUND HQ — TUBE

Steed listens carefully. In distance, a faint sound echoes. A mysterious roar, growing louder...

Louder. And louder... Metal vibrates. But nothing happens. Then Steed looks upwards to see:

POV STEED: *above him* WINDOWS *start to blow, exploding one by one from top down, descending towards him. Glass shards plummet, cascading —*

towards him. Quickly Steed pops umbrella up, as hail of debris thunders over. Windows continue to blow, he has to think fast —

FROM POD —

EMMA'S POV: *thru windows, assumes the worst, looks out to see —*

OUTSIDE TUBE

STEED *hanging from side, swinging over void, buffeted by elements. Inside debris thunders past. Narrow escape. Steed has to haul himself back —*

INSIDE TUBE

Where STEED *looks* FURTHER DOWN, *see stairs end —*

EXT. LONDON — CONTINUOUS ACTION — NIGHT

ON BIG BEN

clock hands tick mercilessly on, as Big Ben's face begins to disintegrate as a lightning storm strikes the structure the faces simultaneously explode.

Biggest cyclone you've ever seen starts slowly whirling above the city, gathering momentum...

NUMBERS *going down, down, down, as...*

INT. UNDERGROUND HQ — CONTROL MODULE

Down in lower glass sphere, SIR AUGUST *supervises controls. Only to hear noise. Sir August turns, as from tower sees —*

STEED

Finally emerge onto catwalk. Sir August grins, relishing encounter.

> SIR AUGUST
> Steed... John Steed. What a horse's
> arse of a name —

> STEED
> No time for pleasantries, Sir

August. We have a score to settle.

SIR AUGUST
I see you found your brolly. Sure
you're up to it, dear boy?

STEED
Absolutely...

Swwiish! Steed unsheathes his umbrella-sword.

Stung, Sir August advances, pouring scorn.

Steed adopts a formal pose, Sir August pauses, half-turns, concealing his hand which, in a blur —

Whoooomm! Pops lethal DARTS at Steed, who — in a flash — lowers BOWLER — ping!! DARTS prick hat like a pin cushion. Crestfallen, Steed checks —

Steed suddenly serious. Now really mad —

STEED
You'll pay for that.

SIR AUGUST
My pleasure.

Beside him, SIR AUGUST picks up STAFF, and —

Blam — ! Swipes a switch. A low growl starts, boosts quickly. As around them, the weather storms start up again —

Now even louder, more violent. ALL HELL BREAKS LOOSE, as Sir August advances with staff, sharp tip gleaming —

On guard. Steed and Sir August close, eyes locked. As numbers grow smaller, they finally meet, and...

The fight is on. Tic-tac-tic... but deadly, as —

SEVERAL ANGLES

up and down catwalk, avoiding weather STORMS —

Tic-tac... Steed and Sir August thrust, parry.

> SIR AUGUST
> Not bad, for a beginner...

> STEED
> I'm not one to boast, Sir August...

> SIR AUGUST
> Hmm... Modest. And much to be
> modest about —

At first, a polite gentlemanly spar. Then more daring, risky... an EPIC
DUEL, *as...*

INTERCUT:

INT. UNDERGROUND HQ — 'POD' —

Inside pod Emma finds herself EXPOSED *to* ELEMENTS...

AHEAD *at centre...*

LIGHTNING *rages at head-height, making her* CROUCH...

She has to CRAWL *along floor until she arrives at...*

CONTROL MECHANISM...

As JOISTS *crack and* BUCKLE...

Emma sees TIMER *racing backwards...*

Stands over SPAGHETTI *wires...*

Emma tries to figure out reconnection. Meanwhile...

DOWN BELOW: *Emma sees other glass sphere...*

REVERSE SHOT: *a tiny Emma right up in the void...*

Between two spheres, hundreds of yards apart... Crackle of
ELECTRIC *energy forces spectacular visible connection. Around
jagged* BOLT, *a storm* HOWLS, *as...*

EMMA *sways in pod control, joists straining, as —*

INTERCUT WITH:

INT. UNDERGROUND HQ — CONTINUOUS ACTION

On end of gantry...

*Tic-tac-tic... Sir August retreats, Steed passes, Sir August cheats,
pushes him back — Steed improvises —*

Tic-tac... Steed redoubles attack, forcing Sir August to defend —

INTERCUT: EMMA *above, swaying in* POD *as weight strains and
weakens joists, battling against storm as —*

Sir August forces Steed up from gantry into —

STAIRWELL

*Tic-tac-tic... duel continues up stairs... Sir August glances up, eyes
gleam, as he mercilessly —*

*Forces Steed up stairs, staff whirling against sword, as Steed
counterattacks —*

> STEED
> Impressive, Sir August. A man of
> rare talents. Such skill...

dedication... utter lunacy —

                  SIR AUGUST
You think I'm mad — ?

                  STEED
I'd settle for 'evil'.

Tic-tac-tic...

                  SIR AUGUST
Time to die.

SIR AUGUST *suddenly* KICKS *at Steed, who loses balance, quickly regaining momentum, as Sir August rushes at him, raining down blows —*

Tic-tac... SIR AUGUST *slashes at Steed's legs, making him* JUMP *up, forcing him to lose balance.*

Steed hangs over edge, looks down, PUSHES *Sir August back. He has to* LEAP —

STEED *thrusts at* SIR AUGUST, *who narrowly dodges, as —*

Up the stairwell, they continue duelling —

INT. UNDERGROUND HQ — 'POD'

EMMA *reaches* CONTROL MECHANISM...

Finds computerized map: operates keyboard to find...

ON SCREEN

Map co-ordinates: lines zero in on Parliament Square: Big Ben. Then a series of commands...

'ANTI-MATTER FISSION 'ON''...

'DISCONNECTION PROCESS: REVEAL CODES'...

ON EMMA/SCREEN

lines of maths code scroll up...

Keeping cool, presses another button — a command:

'MANUAL OVERRIDE... PLEASE WAIT'...

Kept waiting, Emma sighs until...

Diagram of spaghetti-like wire circuit flashes up:

INT. UNDERGROUND HQ — CONTINUOUS ACTION

Meanwhile, at end of stairwell, DUEL *now reaches critical stage of all-out violence...*

Tic-tac-tic... Sir August redoubles attack, forcing Steed out onto catwalk —

Tic-tac... Steed defends, SLAMS *door into Sir August, who emerges full of resolve.*

ON HIGH CATWALK —

Eyes lock. Deadly serious. Tic-tac-tic... A furious blur — tic-tac-tic — Steed presses home advantage, a magnificent final display forces Sir August back —

Who turns suddenly. And in lightning-fast move, flicks his staff, and —

Biff! Whacks Steed's sword out of his hands. Steed watches alarmed as his —

Sword falls DOWN *into void, vanishing, apparently into water, as now inspired —*

Sir August scents victory, viciously whacks Steed down onto ground and using razor-sharp points —

Swissshh! Stabs and slashes at Steed, tearing clothes, as he has to retreat along catwalk, into corner, from where, coiled like a spring —

Steed LEAPS *back up —* GRABS *the* STAFF *— now facing Sir August eye to eye — they struggle — with grim determination Steed tries to wrestle control —*

Sir August fights back, refusing to give, now they trade punches, until Sir August wrests staff free —

Whack! Bats Steed with staff, sending

STEED

Over side of catwalk, DOWN *into the void —*

Spinning down onto —

Slammmm!! Lower catwalk.

FROM EMMA'S SPHERE

Emma sees Steed fall as...

Control POD rocks and rolls...

Emma finally has final three WIRES *poised to connect. She picks two, hesitates —*

> EMMA
> Red... or was it black?

SIR AUGUST *leaps down onto gantry...*

Staff aloft, he closes in on STEED, *almost out —*

RAISES STAFF HIGH

pointing up to heavens like a wizard's wand. Relishes Steed's imminent demise, moves down gantry —

> SIR AUGUST
> "... We are such stuff
> As dreams are made of; and our
> little life is rounded with a sleep..."
> *(Beat)*
> Goodnight, dear...

About to BRING STAFF DOWN *on* STEED, *as —*

Steed stares up at Sir August, from corner of eye, he sees —

Umbrella handle — hanging from rail — trapped by stray cable where it fell —

UP IN POD

About to drop, Emma takes a chance, bets on red, one final go...

> EMMA
> Here goes. Eeny-meeny-miny...

She CONNECTS *two wires together, and —*

Craacccccckkk!! A huge surge of energy LEAPS OUT...

As Sir August bears down, almost upon Steed —

STEED *reaches for sword-umbrella —*

He grabs it, stands up —

SIR AUGUST *backs up as* STEED *advances, and —*

Like twin dervishes — sword against staff —

They go at it, breakneck speed, weapons blurred —

Until STEED *gains upper hand, shows his invincibility —*

And in one fluid move —

Whhooomm — !

Drives swordstick into Sir August —

Who stops dead in tracks, staff raised high like a wizard's wand. In agony, disbelieving —

Craccckkkk!! A huge surge of energy KNOCKS *him back...*

The electrical force fuses a MASSIVE *ball of...*

Prospero-style storm that SWIRLS *and* FIZZES *sending...*

A spectacular lightning BOLT *zapping down and*

CONNECTS

WITH *Sir August's raised* HAND...

Visibly ZIG-ZAGGING *thru his entire body...*

Electrifying him in an instant —

SIR AUGUST *screams out — is* HELD *in the flow of wild natural energy — until well and truly* FRIED *—*

Booomm!! SIR AUGUST *is sucked back into the vortex, vanishing into the storm, as —*

Steed looks up to see —

POD *explodes — !!*

Emma leaps back, stands up, arches limbs...

DIVES OVER SIDE...

A cool, perfect '10' dive thru VOID...

Energy bolts surrounds her in electric slipstream...

POD *joists finally crack, it falls...*

Tumbling thru VOID, *as...*

Thru flames, Emma dives...

Spllllaaasshhh!

INTO WATERS *blow...*

Thru flames POD *falls, crashes into water.*

Steed heads down to help...

INT. UNDERGROUND HQ — CONTINUOUS ACTION

Red numbers freeze...

Inside, weather STORMS die down, SIRENS subside...

EXT. LONDON — CONTINUOUS ACTION — NIGHT

The giant cyclone begins to break apart...

SEVERAL ANGLES — DYING STORM

Outside, storm begins to clear...

CLOSE UP — RELIEVED FACES

INT. UNDERGROUND HQ — CATWALKS

Steed turns, grabs beam for support. Looks down, as —

Swoooshhh!! EMMA *leaps up* FROM WATER, *lungs bursting, gasping for air. Amid flames, he scrambles down to her, helps her out of the water... as* ALARM STILL SOUNDS

STEED

Mrs Peel —

EMMA

What kept you?

Emma looks up. A smile...

They scramble onto catwalk...

Then from behind EMMA...

An ominous CLICK-CLICKING *as*

The PROGRAM *reconfigures...*

Beeeeeep!! goes and the words:

'AUTO-DESTRUCT, 10 SECONDS'

Start flashing...

ON INTERCOM *automatic* VOICE *echoes command, as...*

A different set of numbers start running backwards...

EMMA

You must be joking...

Steed and Emma look at each other.

STEED
And I thought you had it all under
control...

CLOSE UP — AUTO-DESTRUCT NUMBERS

Racing backwards as...

IN SLOW MOTION — *to zero, nothing to stop them...*

With no sound except... TICK-TOCK OF SECOND HAND...

SEVERAL ANGLES

3-2-1 —

BOOOOOOOOOMMMMMMMMM!!!!!!!

inside underground HQ, BLAST *like a nuclear* EXPLOSION —

INT. UNDERGROUND HQ

Woooooommphhhh!!! The firestorm RIPPLES *thru*

The vast inner chamber...

The glass dome...

The Doric columned space...

The endless corridors...

The walls and masonry crumble...

The glass shatters...

The columns collapse...

In Poe-like destruction of Prospero's cave...

EXT. HYDE PARK — SERPENTINE — DAWN

All is calm... until slowly...

Water ripples, leaves on trees shake, as...

From far beneath the earth, like a nuclear test site...

BOOOOOOOOMMMMMMM!!!!!

Explosion reaches surface... a huge FIREBALL *belched out of water, spewing* DEBRIS *up into sky, pluming up thru mushroom of* SMOKE *and* ELECTRIC STATIC...

Heading right up INTO CLOUDS...

Slowly atmospheric colors transform into virulent Turner sky, as if cleansing of all poisons... The trails of FIREBALL...

Drift away, reasserting familiar London skies...

EXT. LONDON — DAWN

Over London, black clouds disappear... a new dawn... sun slowly rising... mare's tail clouds streak sky... snow melts...

EXT. RIVER — DAWN

On Thames... calm of river broken by...

Woooosshhh!! A giant BUBBLE *wooshes up from below, bobbing up on water...* STEED *and* EMMA *inside — before subsiding gently, floating downriver, where —*

INT. MINISTRY — DAWN

Mother, Brenda and staff in the war room. Action stations at an end, emergency over. Cake and macaroons for tea. Outside window, river Thames floats past...

> MOTHER
> *(On hotline)*
> Yes, sir. Confirm reports the storm
> is dropping... Spot of internal
> trouble. I took a firm grip. One or
> two casualties. No word from our
> people yet... Thank you, sir...
> *(Puts phone down; to Brenda)*
> Pity about Steed and Mrs Peel.

> BRENDA
> Missing in action?

> MOTHER
> Better send out a search party... You
> never can tell...

UP AT WINDOW —

look out at Thames... CAMERA goes right up to GLASS, THRU outside into water... UP, UP, UP... until...

EXT. RIVER — DAWN

On surface, bobbing along... the BUBBLE...

Inside Bubble, bodies close. Emma and Steed.

> STEED
> "The owl and the pussycat went to
> sea —"

> EMMA
> "... In a beautiful pea green boat..."

> STEED
> A fine night, Mrs Peel. Just a bit
> chilly. I think we deserve some
> champagne...

Emma intrigued. Alone together, as the Bubble drifts downstream...

SLOW DISSOLVE TO:

EXT. STEED'S RESIDENCE — ROOFTOP — DAY

CLOSE UP*: Champagne bottle on ice —*

On Steed's rooftop, freak weather: a bright shaft of sun beats down on his formal roof garden, sending temperatures soaring.

> EMMA (O.S.)
> I don't recall London being this
> warm, Steed.

STEED, EMMA *and* MOTHER *together in sun, reclining on Steed's rooftop in exotic summer outfits.*

> STEED
> Wonderland Weather, Mrs Peel. The
> latest thing. I made an early
> booking.

CLOSE UP*:* POP! *champagne cork pops, bubbles spilling from bottle —*

> MOTHER
> Champagne?

> EMMA
> Please.

STEED

Of course.

MOTHER

A toast.
                    (Raises his glass)
To a job well done.

They raise glasses together.

PULL BACK REVEALS: REST OF LONDON *in* GREY GLOOM

EMMA

To a narrow escape.

STEED

I did have him, of course...

EMMA

Did you.

STEED

Mrs Peel, if I say I had him...

MOTHER

Ahem... Macaroon?

Laughter. CHINK *of glasses.*

EMMA

Thank you, Steed.

STEED

No. Thank you, Mrs Peel.

FADE TO BLACK

the avengers

the making of the movie
DAVE ROGERS

the avengers

BY JULIE KAEWERT BASED ON THE ORIGINAL SCREENPLAY BY DON MACPHERSON

THE AVENGERS
COMPANION

over **100** colour photographs

ALAIN CARRAZÉ & JEAN-LUC PUTHEAUD

THE AVENGERS COMPANION
A complete guide to the classic television series
By Alain Carrazé and Jean-Luc Putheaud

Swinging sixties London, bowler hats and leather boots,
catsuits and karate kicks — it has to be the quintessentially
British wit and style of *The Avengers*.

In this lavishly illustrated companion to the original, stylish
sixties cult television show, you can read exclusive
interviews with Patrick Macnee (John Steed), Diana Rigg
(Emma Peel) and Linda Thorson (Tara King), plus *Avengers*
creator Brian Clemens, and discover for yourself the
enduring appeal of the show.

Accompanied by hundreds of rare photos, many in colour,
there are overviews and episode guides for all 161 *Avengers*
and all 26 *New Avengers* episodes, plus features on the
Avengers' key adversaries, the Cybernauts, actor biographies,
articles on *Avengers* vehicles and a tribute to the *Avengers'*
fashion style.

**'Sumptuous! A glossy and well-designed
pictorial treat.' — *SFX***

To order by credit card, phone 01536 763 631

THE
AVENGERS
AND ME

PATRICK MACNEE
WITH DAVE ROGERS

Also available from Titan Books

THE AVENGERS AND ME

By Patrick Macnee with Dave Rogers

For the first time, Patrick Macnee tells all! The behind-the-scenes secrets of the classic television series *The Avengers* are laid bare by the man who *was* John Steed. In unflinching detail, Macnee reveals the true story behind *The Avengers*, including his relationships with all four *Avengers* girls — on *and* off the set. Honor Blackman and her kinky boots, Diana Rigg as Emma Peel, Linda Thorson as Tara King, onto Joanna Lumley and *The New Avengers*, and even an appearance with Oasis, Macnee witnessed it all.

Lavishly illustrated, with many rare and previously unpublished pictures from Macnee's private collection, and with contributions by fellow *Avengers* actors, directors, producers and screenwriters, this is a unique history of the trials and triumphs of a series as popular today as when it was first screened.

'Charming... Hats off to you, sir!' — *Uncut*

'A frank, unmissable read.' — *SFX*

To order by credit card, phone 01536 763 631